I resonated with *Aslan's Breath* from page one. Dicke[...] deep and clear are C.S. Lewis's theological wells. Moreover, ne shows how natural it is to read Narnia as a work of spiritual theology in the school of Eugene Peterson, where we think Christianly about living fully and well in Lewis's great writing project. *Aslan's Breath* benefits from the care, creativity, and wisdom of Dickerson's personal journey of reading the Narniad. The result is a book that will allow the magical worlds of Narnia to live and breathe in fresh new ways for the imaginative reader.
—BRENTON DICKIESON, curator of *A Pilgrim In Narnia*

I've read lots of books that unpack spiritual themes in Narnia: this one is different. Rather than offering a wide catalog of observations, Dickerson dives deep into one key concept: portrayals of the Holy Spirit. The result? Not only substantial insight into Narnia but a practical vision of ways to welcome that same Spirit into our daily lives. This is a very good book, and, I think, an important one.
—DIANA PAVLAC GLYER, author of *Bandersnatch: C.S. Lewis, J.R.R. Tolkien, and the Creative Collaboration of the Inklings*

Curl up with your Narnia collection, your Bible, and a very large cup of tea for this one: reading *Aslan's Breath* felt like leaning into Aslan's back and hearing him purr. For Narnia devotees and first time readers alike, Matthew's book will bring "aha!" moments and deeper, more joyful understanding of Lewis's intent. As we delve deeply into the meaning of Aslan's breath, we learn more about the Holy Spirit's work and play among us. I found myself laughing, sometimes moved to tears, and writing notes all through it. What a rich read.
—KATY BOWSER HUTSON, author of *Now I Lay Me Down To Fight*

Through a close and sensitive reading of all seven volumes, Matthew Dickerson explores how the Chronicles of Narnia illuminate the biblical understanding of the person and work of the Holy Spirit. In our often individualistic, hectic, and fear-filled world, *Aslan's Breath* helps us to better prepare ourselves to hear the vital promptings of the Holy Spirit. Carefully, personably, speaking with his readers as if we were sitting with the author in his living room, or joining him on a hike, Dickerson inspires us to receive God-breathed courage and hope, to live God-anointed lives.

—MONIKA B. HILDER, Professor of English, Trinity Western University; author of *The Gender Dance: Ironic Subversion in C. S. Lewis's Cosmic Trilogy* and *Letters to Annie*

Do the Chronicles of Narnia stand alone as story? Of course. Do they also benefit from thoughtful exploration of their theological themes? Definitely. In this book, Matthew Dickerson goes beyond the pious platitudes some have drawn from Narnia and digs into the meat of the story looking for the Holy Spirit. And, in a careful and close reading of the text of all seven Chronicles, Dickerson finds Him. This book will illuminate your own readings (and hopefully frequent rereadings) of Narnia. Take it as a guide next time you plunge in.

—JENNIFER WOODRUFF TAIT, senior editor, *Christian History* magazine, and author of *Christian History in Seven Sentences*

How seldom, these days, do we meet with books that are genuine friends for the journey. In the pages of *Aslan's Breath,* we find an author's voice that is conversational and winsome-—a presence that comes alongside the reader. Matthew Dickerson knows the realm of Narnia very well indeed, and shares many an insight that brings richness to walking the paths of this good country.

An air of discovering pervades this excellent book. What's more, and what is best—the gift of C.S. Lewis' writing about the Holy Spirit, amid scenes of comfort, re-assurance, and peace, shines in this book. So, in these pages, we've a true gift: one that illumines the seven books of the Narnian Chronicles.

—KEVIN BELMONTE, historian, and biographer of William Wilberforce, G.K. Chesterton, and John Bunyan

ASLAN'S BREATH

Seeing the
Holy Spirit
in Narnia

MATTHEW DICKERSON

Illustrated by Ned Bustard

In Christian art, the square halo identified a living person presumed to be a saint. Square Halo Books is devoted to publishing works that present contextually sensitive biblical studies and practical instruction consistent with the Doctrines of the Reformation. The goal of Square Halo Books is to provide materials useful for encouraging and equipping the saints.

©2024 Square Halo Books, Inc.
P.O. Box 18954
Baltimore, MD 21206
www.SquareHaloBooks.com

ISBN 978-1-941106-33-4
Library of Congress Control Number: 2023942519

Printed in the United States of America

In memory of
Leslie Anne Bustard
(1968–2023)

And with that he breathed on them
and said, "Receive the Holy Spirit."
—John 20:22

[God is] brought boldly into a community of
men, women, and children who are called
to enter into this communal life of love,
an emphatically personal life where they
experience themselves in personal terms of
love and forgiveness, of hope and desire.
Under the image of the Trinity we discover
that we do not know God by defining him
but by being loved by him and loving in return.
—Eugene Peterson

CONTENTS

An Origin Story

A few years ago, I saw a post by one of my social media friends. I don't remember the exact wording, but the gist of it was as follows:

> Lewis was a Trinitarian Christian. He believed in a triune God: one God in the three persons of Father, Son, and Holy Spirit. In the seven volumes of the Chronicles of Narnia and its otherworldly fantasy setting, Lewis seems to represent God the Son most clearly in the great lion Aslan. God the Father is also present in the Emperor-beyond-the-Sea, the father of Aslan. But that's only two persons of the Trinity. We might also expect to see the Holy Spirit present or represented in Narnia. *Do the Narnia stories have any pointers to the Third Person of the Trinity? If so, where and what are they?*

This book is an exploration of those last two questions. To remove all suspense (if there was any) my answer to the first of these questions is "yes" and my answer to the second is given in the title of this book—though, as we shall see, that's only the start of the answer.

Some might describe this relationship between Aslan and Christ as allegorical, others as mythological, still others as symbolic or metaphorical. Some might suggest it is a combination of these. How readers see the

relationship between Christ and the literary figure of Aslan, is not as important (to this book) as the fact that there is a relationship. As Jesus came into
our world incarnate as a human in flesh and blood, so also Aslan appears in
Narnia incarnate as a talking beast (i.e., as one of the Narnian creatures whom
he helped create), dies a sacrificial death on the Stone Table and is resurrected.
Once a connection is made between Aslan and the person of Jesus (the incarnate Son of God, and Second Person of the Trinity), it is not difficult to recognize
a connection between God the Father and Aslan's father, the Emperor-beyond-the-Sea.

A similar point can be made that there is a relationship between the Holy
Spirit and Aslan's Breath—whether one speaks of it as allegory, mythology,
or imagery. And that's all readers need to know from this introduction. Feel
free to jump to Chapter 1 (as though stepping directly into Narnia through a
wardrobe or picture frame). Those interested in a brief account of the origins
of this book, and an initial defense of why Lewis would have chosen the image
of Aslan's breath, should continue on with this introduction (which may be like
journeying to Narnia via the Wood Between the Worlds, where almost nothing
happens—unless you happen to be there at just the right time to see a pond
appear as a world is born, or a pond dry up as a world dies).

ONE POSSIBLE ANSWER

The New Testament accounts suggest one possible answer. Jesus made
several bodily appearances over the forty days between his resurrection and
ascension. The Gospels of Matthew and John name Mary Magdalene as the
first to have seen him. John also mentions that Jesus' third appearance took
place on the shore of the Sea of Galilee and included a miraculously provided
meal of fish and bread (John 21:1–14). Paul adds that Jesus appeared to more
than five hundred persons during this period (1 Corinthians 15:3-7). Then, as
Luke's Gospel tells us, Jesus ascended to Heaven (Luke 24:50–51). Ten days after
the ascension, on the day of Pentecost, the Holy Spirit came as promised and
remained in and with Christ's disciples—not only on Pentecost, but throughout
the rest of history. *There is no biblical record of Jesus appearing again in bodily
form after his ascension and after Pentecost.*

That last point is the important one. Although Stephen, just before he was martyred, was filled with the Holy Spirit and had a vision of Jesus (Acts 7:55–56), he described Jesus as being in Heaven "standing at the right hand of God" and not in bodily form on earth. A little later, Jesus spoke to Paul on the road to Damascus (Acts 9:1–9), but he was present only as a blinding light and a voice. We also read of "the Lord" (understood to be Jesus) speaking to Paul in Corinth (Acts 18:9–10), but this appearance is explicitly described as a vision. Likewise, when Paul told the crowds in Jerusalem what the Lord told him (Acts 22:17–21), he described the experience as being in a "trance." The Book of Revelation describes an encounter of Apostle John with Jesus, but as with the previous examples Jesus was with John (or John was with Jesus) in an apocalyptic vision and not in bodily form on earth. It is only when the Lord stands beside Paul during his trial before the Sanhedrin (Acts 23:11) that Luke's wording does not explicitly describe the appearance as a vision. In that instance, however, Paul is a prisoner in a Roman barracks with no mention of anybody else seeing Jesus. Most commentators understand this also as a vision of Jesus and not a bodily appearance.[1]

Like Jesus, Aslan also has a brief period following his resurrection when he is bodily present in Narnia and interacts with Narnians in much the same physical way he did before his death. These appearances take place in the final three chapters of *The Lion, the Witch and the Wardrobe*. Aslan first appears to Lucy and Susan, who had been attempting to care for his body after his death (as two named women sought to do for Jesus after his death). Then he travels to the castle of the White Witch where he restores to life many creatures whom the witch had turned to stone. Presumably, those restored creatures will later appear to their loved ones and to others in Narnia. With the exception of Tumnus's reunion with Lucy, those moments are not described in the narrative. Yet readers might imagine scenes a bit like the dead rising from their tombs and

---

1   In Acts 10, Peter had a vision in which a voice speaks to him (three times) telling him to eat that which had previous been unclean. He addressed the voice as KYRIE (10:14) which can mean "master" or "lord." Although this title was sometimes used to address Jesus, Peter does not use the title THEOS (God). Luke identifies the voice that earlier spoke to the Roman centurion Cornelius as an angel of the Lord (10:3). In any case, if it was Jesus who spoke to Peter, this also took place in a vision and also involved only a voice.

appearing to many in Jerusalem after the death of Jesus (Matthew 27:51–53)—although the statues *remain* alive after Aslan resurrects them. With this newly awakened multitude, Aslan proceeds to the battle-in-progress where he defeats the witch and is seen alive and in the flesh (and fur) by many more Narnians including Peter and Edmund. Like Jesus, Aslan then provides food for his followers in a seemingly miraculous way. They journey together to Cair Paravel, and three days after his resurrection Aslan presides over the coronation of the four Pevensies where again he is seen by numerous Narnians.

Then he quietly slips away. Nobody knows exactly when or where, and nobody follows him. Those who have read the other books in the Chronicles of Narnia may well guess that Aslan has gone to Aslan's Country, where he dwells in close fellowship with his Father, the Emperor—and where characters (and readers) meet him in *The Voyage of the Dawn Treader* and *The Silver Chair*, and in a different way in *The Last Battle*. The coronation scene is, in a way, Aslan's ascension moment.

Amid the numerous parallels between the accounts of Jesus and Lewis's story of Aslan, there is one striking difference, and that might be a hint as to where to look for the Holy Spirit in Narnia. Unlike Jesus, Aslan does appear in Narnia again in the flesh on multiple occasions! In the final chapter of *The Lion, the Witch and the Wardrobe,* the four Pevensie children remember Mr. Beaver's words about Aslan: "He'll be coming and going. One day you'll see him and another you won't. He doesn't like being tied down—and of course he has other countries to attend to. It's quite all right. He'll often drop in. Only you mustn't press him. He's wild, you know. Not like a *tame* lion." That is a good description of at least some of the books set in Narnia after this time. Since Jesus no longer appears on earth after his ascension, but the Holy Spirit has remained present with followers of Christ, those looking for close connections between the Narnia stories and the Church story might suppose Lewis represented the Holy Spirit in Narnia through those later (post- resurrection and post-coronation) appearances of Aslan.

Following this hint in considering the physical appearances of Aslan in Narnia as possible pointers to the Holy Spirit, we are only interested in the post-resurrection, post-coronation appearances. Thus, we don't count *The

Magician's Nephew or *The Lion, the Witch and the Wardrobe*; those stories take place prior to Aslan's death on the Stone Table. Neither should we count Aslan's appearances in his own country—for example at the start and end of *The Silver Chair*, the end of the *Voyage of the Dawn Treader*, or the end of *The Last Battle*. These are not appearances *in Narnia*; they function more like a portrayal of Jesus in Heaven at the right hand of the throne of God, perhaps akin to John's visions of Jesus in Revelation.

What are Aslan's other appearances outside his own country? On at least two occasions, he appears in what is explicitly described as a vision or dream: first to Caspian (in the final chapter of *The Voyage of the Dawn Treader*), and later to Jill in "The House of Harfang" (Chapter 8 of *The Silver Chair*). Aslan's earlier appearance to Caspian, Edmund, Lucy, and Reepicheep on Deathwater Island (Chapter 8 of *The Voyage of the Dawn Treader*) is somewhat ambiguous, but a few descriptions of this appearance also make it seem more like a dream than like a physical appearance: there is a bright light (as with Jesus' appearance to Saul on the road to Damascus); Aslan is much too large even by his own standards of largeness; he does not get close enough to be touched or to have any physical interaction; he does not speak; the whole appearance lasts only a paragraph and then Aslan disappears; and the narrator describes all who saw him as "like people waking from a sleep" who (like Jill in Harfang) later seem to have no memory of the appearance. In each of these visions, Aslan gives guidance or prompts the consciences of the characters to turn away from some evil. Voices and promptings of conscience and guidance certainly remind us of the work of the Holy Spirit in our lives, lending credence to the idea that latter appearances of Aslan function as pointers to the Holy Spirit.

But what about actual bodily appearances? In *The Voyage of the Dawn Treader*, Aslan is physically present (and not merely in a dream or vision) with Lucy in the house of Coriakin (Chapter 10). However, he is invisible throughout most of that scene, and Lucy doesn't even know he is there. After he is made visible, he tells Lucy, "I have been here all the time," but shortly after that he "instantly ... vanished away." Neither Edmund nor Eustace nor Caspian get to see him on the Island of the Voices. And though he tells Lucy that he is going to visit Trumpkin (suggesting another bodily appearance of Aslan in Narnia), readers are not invited to that meeting and don't know what form it takes. This might also remind us of what we learn of the Holy Spirit in John 3:8: that he is present and active (like the wind), but not visible to our eyes. A similar observation could be made when Aslan is first present with Lucy, Susan, Edmund, Peter, and Trumpkin in *Prince Caspian*: he is invisible to at least some of them. Though the narrator lets readers know that Aslan is there, many of the characters in the story don't see him. Even Lucy, who believes he is there, at times only catches glimpses of him. All these examples might support the idea that Aslan's latter appearances in Narnia function as pointers to the *work* of the Holy Spirit if not to the Holy Spirit himself.

On the other hand, we might also note that the dream appearances of Aslan also bear something in common with the visions Paul and John had of Jesus. While these examples might be a *part* of how Lewis reveals to readers something of the work of the Holy Spirit (an idea to which we will return in the final chapter), in terms of a symbolic, allegorical, or mythological portrayal of the Holy Spirit in Narnia, this answer still seems unsatisfying to me for a few reasons.

One is that while the idea might fit a few of Aslan's post-resurrection appearances, there are others for which it doesn't fit well at all. These include Aslan's later appearances in *Prince Caspian* and his appearances in *The Horse and His Boy*. After he reveals himself to Trumpkin in *Prince Caspian,* Aslan is very much a physical and visible presence in Narnia, even allowing Lucy and Susan to ride on his back. This prolonged appearance seems much more like those of Aslan in *The Lion, the Witch and the Wardrobe*. Likewise, Aslan's appearances in *The Horse and His Boy* have more in common with his previous incarnate form—more like how Jesus used to walk with his disciples than like how the Holy Spirit is described in the New Testament or is experienced by those who have received the Spirit.

My biggest objection, though, is that this would conflate the Second and Third persons of the Trinity. The Trinitarian doctrine affirms one God but three persons. God the Son and God the Holy Spirit are different persons of the Trinity. To have both represented by the same *physical* body of Aslan would be less satisfying in a literary way (at least to me).

Granted that these objections might all come from trying to force the Narnia stories into too strict of an allegorical mold, or to cram too much into a symbol. All such symbols ultimately are only that: symbols which fail to fully reflect that toward which they point. On one hand we might miss something by forcing it *too much* into strict allegory, but on the other hand we also might miss something if we reject an idea because it does not fit *enough* as allegory.

ASLAN'S BREATH: A BETTER ANSWER?

In any case, I think there is a better answer: the one suggested by the title of this book, and also by its epigraph. It is an answer right in front of us in the language of Scripture and the language of the Narnia stories. Or, we might say, in the langua*ges* of Scripture: both the Hebrew of the Old Testament and the Greek of the New Testament.

In biblical Hebrew, the word *ruach* can be translated in modern English as "spirit," with the phrase *ruach elohim* most often rendered as "Spirit of God." We see the phrase *ruach elohim* at the start of Scripture in Genesis 1:2 , which the NIV translates as "The spirit of God was hovering over the waters." However, scholars of ancient Hebrew tell us that *ruach* can also mean "breath" or "wind." We must understand from context which of these possible meanings—*spirit, breath,* or *wind,* or perhaps even something more mysterious that incorporates all of them—is intended . Thus, in some other passages the NIV translates *ruach* as *breath* (for example, Job 12:10) or *wind* (for example, in Numbers 11:31). While nearly all English translations translate *ruach elohim* in Genesis 1:2 as "Spirit of God," the Common English Bible (CEB) renders the second phrase of Genesis 1:2 as "God's wind swept over the waters."

Similarly, the New Testament Greek word translated as *spirit* (for example in the John 3 passage mentioned above) is a form of *pneuma* which can also mean *breath* or *wind.* It is from this word that we get modern English words like *pneumatic* (which describes something running on the power of air) or *pneumonia* (an illness which impacts our breathing). When Jesus speaks to Nicodemus in the John 3 dialogue describing the need to be "born again"—to be born of the Spirit as well as the flesh—he uses wind as a metaphor for spirit, saying, "The wind blows wherever it pleases. You hear its sound, but you cannot tell where

it comes from or where it is going. So it is with everyone born of the Spirit"
(John 3:8). Jesus was most likely speaking Aramaic, but John writes his Gospel
account in Greek, using the same word *pneuma* for both "wind" and "Spirit"—
though the latter is in the possessive form to indicate "of the Spirit." (Translators
typically choose to translate the first occurrence of the word as "wind" in this
case because it is associated with the verb "blow," as well as from the sentence
structure which suggests a metaphor.) Many other New Testament passages use
the title *pneuma hagion* meaning Holy Spirit (which would also distinguish this
from the use of *pneuma* to mean "breath" or "wind.")

So we see that in both New Testament Greek and the Hebrew of the Old
Testament the Spirit of God—that is, the Holy Spirit: the Third Person of the
Trinity—is also (in its linguistic roots) the Breath of God (or even the Wind of
God). C.S. Lewis was fluent in Greek. On multiple occasions, he commented on
the meanings of Greek words used in the New Testament, including variations
of meaning between similar words. One of his many beloved books is *The Four
Loves,* which explores four types of love represented by different Greek words
with subtle (or not-so- subtle) variations in meaning, and yet all of which (unfortunately) often get translated to the single English word *love.* For one looking
for the Holy Spirit in Narnia, "breath"—in particular, the breath of Aslan—is a
good place to start.

The idea that Aslan's breath might represent either the Holy Spirit or Aslan's
imparting of his spirit becomes even more compelling when we consider the
post-resurrection passage John 20:21 – 22 that provides the epigraph to this book.
"Again Jesus said, 'Peace be with you! As the Father has sent me, I am sending you.'
And with that he breathed on them and said, 'Receive the Holy Spirit.'" Jesus was
using the same imagery that is suggested in the languages of the Bible, associating breath with spirit—though here John uses a different word, *enephuseés,* for
the phrase "breathed on them" while using *pneuma hagion* for Holy Spirit. Given
how much New Testament imagery Lewis draws on in his telling of the Narnia
stories, might we not expect him to use the same imagery we see in John 20? As
it is in Jesus' act of breathing on his disciples that they receive the Holy Spirit, it
seems quite reasonable—expected, even—that we would find in Aslan's breath on

his followers a pointer to the Holy Spirit in Narnia.

Surprisingly, when I looked through numerous books on my shelf exploring the writings of C.S. Lewis, I found none that mentioned Aslan's breath in relation to the Holy Spirit. Yet the more I looked at examples of Aslan's breath in the Narnia stories, the more it seemed to me that this was exactly what C.S. Lewis was doing—perhaps unconsciously at first, but consciously later on. Eventually, my searches of literature uncovered an abstract of an article mentioning the idea. So I was saved (I thought) from having to write my own essay on the topic. Still, I filed my thoughts away for a possible future talk.

That "future talk" came a few years later, in March of 2023, when the New York C.S. Lewis Society invited me to speak at their monthly meeting. It was my third time speaking to the group. The previous two years I had presented something I considered a more "scholarly" exploration from one of my published books or book chapters. In 2023, however, I suggested "Aslan's Breath" as my topic, stating it would not be an academic or scholarly talk, but just a few reflections on Lewis's portrayal of the Holy Spirit in the Chronicles of Narnia. Of course, once I set the title and date, I had to prepare the talk. Which is why I agreed to do it: as a means of pushing myself into the exploration, forcing me to think carefully about the idea and to delve into the related passages. As I did so, an interesting thing happened. As I looked over several relevant passages in the weeks leading up to the presentation—passages from the Chronicles of Narnia as well as from the Bible—I not only became more convinced that Lewis was indeed portraying the Holy Spirit in Narnia especially through Aslan's breath, but also that his portrayal yielded meaningful insights into the work of the Holy Spirit and was even more subtle, complex, and multifaceted than I originally imagined. Perhaps it was even worth a deeper exploration. By the time I finished preparing the talk, I had begun to think there was enough material to fill not just an essay or article, but even a short book.

At the end of my presentation, many members of the society agreed and encouraged me to do just that: to put my ideas into a book. I am deeply thankful to them for that encouragement! Without it, I might never have written this.

LITERARY SPIRITUAL THEOLOGY
(AND GOALS FOR THIS BOOK)

In the following chapters we will look through the entirety of the Chronicles of Narnia at every reference to Aslan's breath (and, as we shall see, also at a few other related passages and images, including Aslan's kiss). In each example, we will see how Lewis might be pointing us toward the Holy Spirit, and what insights we might gain from those pointers. The book is arranged around the seven volumes in the order in which they were published, one chapter devoted to each book.

When I write about literature—especially the literature I love most dearly, which includes the fiction of C.S. Lewis and J.R.R. Tolkien—I nearly always come to the task with two primary motivations. The first is that I am interested in a close reading of the texts. This brings me back to my college freshman English course on *Paradise Lost* with the late Professor Marion Singleton. I owe her a great debt for helping me develop a delight in reading literature carefully and for teaching me how to write about it. A few weeks before I began this introduction, I was speaking about J.R.R. Tolkien's short autobiographical allegorical fairy tale "Leaf by Niggle" at a conference in Texas. Afterward, somebody told me they appreciated my "sensitive reading." That was one of the most encouraging things I could have been told. Reading literature does involve our imagination. It requires imaginative insights. Yet the danger I always want to avoid is forcing something into a work that is not there: pushing my own ideas into the words rather than seeking the mind of the author or the meanings present in the words themselves. Approaching literature with humility seems to me to be central to the task of a reader, especially one who hopes to write about that literature. And that is also how we should approach Scripture: seeking to understand and engage our imagination while also approaching the text with humility. Since it is the author's own thoughts I hope to understand, it is always the primary texts I want to focus on.

Not that I don't appreciate scholarly work. I have learned a great deal over the years from the research and writings of numerous scholars who have closely studied the writings of C.S. Lewis and J.R.R. Tolkien. In the past, I have written

several books and book chapters which have benefited greatly from that scholarship. I even like to think that my own writings have added to that scholarship,
helping (and being enjoyed by) others! But I will not be delving into that scholarship in this book. My goal is more personal. As I told the New York C.S. Lewis
Society, this work is not intended as an academic, scholarly, or research work.
For the sake of brevity and readability[2], I do not cite any of the large volumes of
C.S. Lewis scholarship in print (though much of it is very worthwhile). The focus
is entirely on the primary texts of the seven Narnia stories. I also don't claim
that I am the first to consider this idea about Aslan's breath, or that my presentation is especially original. There are other writers and scholars of Lewis's
works who could do a better job of that.

In many ways, this leads me to my second motivation for writing about
literature: its applicability to life. Countless questions may surface about any
given work of literature that, while interesting to some and perhaps of scholarly
import, are not relevant to what I think of as the deepest questions. (I think, for
example, of a debate over whether the waistcoat of Smaug the dragon was a
literal one—like the waistcoat Bilbo Baggins wore—or a metaphorical one. It's
a fun question to consider. But it's not one, as far as I can see, that gets at J.R.R.
Tolkien's moral vision, or his explorations of the meaning of art and creativity in
the face of mortality.) I am more drawn to the questions that explore what the

---

2   Even to start down that path of more traditional scholarship would immediately change the tone
    of this book. That approach might indeed make this a better work (at least for some), but it would
    make a *different* book. My attention would quickly be at least partly diverted from the primary
    works of C.S.Lewis to the secondary works *about* Lewis. And if I research and cite even a single
    scholarly source, the expectation is that I will cite several sources: that the book would indeed
    fill with citations to *all* the scholarly work that has been written about C.S.Lewis—or at least a
    large amount of it. (And here I must confess at least my own prideful experience of opening
    up books about topics I have written about, and looking for references to my works among the
    various citations—and being annoyed if my books are not referenced. I also confess the pride of
    wanting to write such a scholarly book that would receive praise and accolades from the many
    scholars whose works I admire. It is a prideful desire I must actively resist.) My own many re-
    peated readings of C.S.Lewis over the past 50 years have led me to certain insights that in some
    ways are not original—in that others have independently had the same insights and in some
    cases have written about them—and yet which came to me without having read those writings.
    In some ways I therefore appreciate the fact that there are many scholarly works that touch on
    the topics of this book that I have *not* read, and which have not directly shaped this book. In any
    case, whatever weaknesses there may be in my approach, I hope that at least some readers will
    find it meaningful and enjoyable. For those desiring a more scholarly exploration, I offer at the
    end of the book a short appendix.

Good Life is and how we live it. How do I avoid becoming like Uncle Andrew? Or Jadis? How do I avoid becoming a dragon (as Eustace did)—or recognizing when I *have* become one (as Eustace also did)? How can I become the sort of person who can see as clearly as Puddleglum did even when the Emerald Witch was doing her best to put him under her spell?

For several years, as I read more than a dozen of his books and had a chance to spend time with him personally, I had heard or read Eugene Peterson's phrase "spiritual theology"—a phrase he used to describe most of his later writings. It was only recently, however, that I came upon his definition of the term in his book *Christ Plays in Ten Thousand Places.* "Spiritual theology is a pair of words that hold together what is so often 'sawn asunder.' It represents the attention that the church community gives to keeping what we think about God (theology) in organic connection with the way we live with God (spirituality)" (4). That captures my interest in Scripture. And it carries over into my interest in literature. I am interested not only in what we should think about Lewis's stories—that is, how to understand them—but in what they can teach us about how to live. That's true of any literature I take the time to write about. Those are the "organic connections" that compel my interest. (Though, admittedly, I do at times wonder about Smaug's waistcoat.)

A little later in the same book, Peterson also notes, "Genesis 1 and 2 have been studied meticulously for two thousand years by some of our very best scholars, Jewish and Christian. The accumulated insights and truths stagger our imaginations. There is so much here to consider and ponder, to appreciate and respond to. It is not possible to over-appreciate these scholars, whether living or dead." If I replaced "two thousand years" with "almost a century," I could write the same thing about C.S. Lewis, and also note how valuable the tremendous scholarship has been, to me in particular and to the world in general. Peterson goes on, however, to say about Genesis 1 and 2, "But what is sometimes missed in this cascade of exegetical brilliance is how skillfully and well these texts prepare and lead each of us as ordinary working Christians.... right now." He describes them as "texts for living in the time and place that we wake up each morning" (63). It is the insights (ironically from works of fantasy) into how we live our ordinary lives right now that most draw me not only to read literature but to write about it. That was the focus with which I wanted to approach Lewis's works. Not to reduce a story to moral lesson or series of moral lessons. That would do grave injustice to the story *as story* and its power to work in our lives in a way that abstract moral principles do not. But simply to explore—without getting caught up in what is admittedly the exegetical brilliance of some of the existing scholarship—how those texts can prepare me to live in the time and place I wake up each morning. And, in particular, to do so in a way more deeply transformed by the Holy Spirit's work in my life.

Even as this book is not intended as a scholarly or academic work on the writings of C.S. Lewis, it is also not intended as a theological treatise on the Holy Spirit. There are already excellent sources exploring this topic. Numerous theologians and biblical scholars could do—and, indeed, have done—a much better job understanding and writing about the Holy Spirit than I could. As already noted, this is a more personal book: the sort of exploration that, the more I went on, the more I got excited about what I was discovering and how rich the material was. Also, how challenging it was to me personally. It is an exploration, I think, with applications to how I am to live my life in the presence, power, knowledge, guidance, and comfort of the Holy Spirit. I hope that for my readers it may provide similar enjoyment as well insights both into how C.S. Lewis's creative literary mind worked, and, more importantly, into how we might better understand the workings of the Holy Spirit.

A final introductory thought: several years ago, after an annual gathering of a writers' group I belong to, my wife and I had the delight of having Eugene and Jan Peterson as our passengers on the two-hour drive from the retreat center back to the airport. Eugene happened to be re-reading the Chronicles of Narnia at the time, and he was full of delight about the insights he was gaining—and how enjoyable and rich the books (and his re-readings of them) were. It was a wonderful conversation! Eugene was already in his mid-70s at the time and had spent a lifetime following Christ, yet he was still learning. And still learning from imaginative literature. I am not nearly as far along my spiritual or literary journey as Eugene was, so it shouldn't have been surprising to me that in the process of writing this book I kept making new discoveries.

I

THE LION, THE WITCH AND THE WARDROBE

Transforming Power

The White Witch has put Aslan to death on the Stone Table. Lucy and Susan have been mourning over his body, even as they vainly sought to untie him. Then along came the mice, who with their teeth did what the girls could not do, freeing Aslan from his bonds. The whole scene is beautiful, powerful, and memorable. And now, just as the red of dawn has turned to gold, the Stone Table has cracked. Aslan has risen from the dead. Lucy and Susan have seen him, and Susan wonders fearfully whether he is a ghost.

Here in Chapter 15, "Deeper Magic from before the Dawn of Time," we read the first reference to Aslan's breath in *The Lion, the Witch and the Wardrobe*. In response to Susan wondering whether he is a ghost, "Aslan stooped his golden head and licked her forehead. The warmth of his breath and a rich sort of smell that seemed to hang about his hair came all over her."

"RECEIVE THE HOLY SPIRIT"

I have read this scene many times. When I returned to it, I at first glance saw nothing particularly deep in terms of the Holy Spirit. It is a moving scene, certainly, especially after the sorrow of Aslan's death at the cruel hands of the White Witch and her followers. Yet is it really a pointer to the Holy Spirit? After all, sometimes a sword really is just a sword, and a cave really is a cave. And a reference to Aslan's breath may signify nothing more than a physical phenomenon: the warm moist air that comes from his mouth when he exhales. We must be careful not to put more into symbols than is there, which also means not to see as symbolic or meta-phorical something which in fact does not signify more than itself.

Still, there is this: although Scripture often alludes to the Spirit of God even before the time of Christ—indeed, from the start of creation in Genesis 1:2—it is shortly after the resurrection of Jesus (on the day of Pentecost) that the Spirit first comes upon all believers. Might we not then expect a reference to the Spirit coming upon Susan also to occur shortly after the resurrection of Aslan? The post-resurrection passage from the end of the Gospel of John (briefly mentioned in the introduction to this book) is even more suggestive of this symbolism. "Again Jesus said, 'Peace be with you! As the Father has sent me, I am sending you.' And with that he breathed on them and said, 'Receive the Holy Spirit'" (John 20:21–22). Reading that passage, it becomes difficult for me *not* to see some suggestion of the Holy Spirit in the act of Aslan breathing on Susan. Another thing worth noting in this passage is that Aslan's breath doesn't merely touch Susan's face, but it comes "all over" her. We might say that it covers her or fills her. An even better description might be that the breath baptizes her. All four Gospels record John the Baptist speaking of Jesus (the promised Messiah) as the one who will come and baptize with the Holy Spirit (Matthew 3:11, Mark 1:8, Luke 3:16, John 1:33). It makes sense, then, that Aslan would be the one to baptize Susan with the Holy Spirit, just as we might expect Lewis to use Aslan's breath as the symbol for the Spirit.

Indeed, Jesus' wonderful and important promise to his disciples is that he will send the Holy Spirit, fulfilling the words that his cousin John the Baptist had spoken of him earlier. John 14:15– 31 records Jesus' most extensive teaching on this topic. Jesus repeats the promise twice in this passage: "And I will ask the Father, and he will give you another advocate to help you and be with you forever—the Spirit of truth" (16–17a); and again, "But the Advocate, the Holy Spirit, whom the Father will send in my name, will teach you all things and will remind you of everything I have said to you" (26). Along with an encouraging word about why the Spirit's coming is so important, Jesus speaks of going away and suggests that the Holy Spirit will only come after he departs and returns to the Father. We see the coming of the Holy Spirit most powerfully on the day of Pentecost which is, indeed, after Jesus has ascended. Yet we also see him breathing on the disciples and telling them to receive the Holy Spirit, which of course happens while he is still present.

Consider also the response of the two girls at this moment. Lucy cries out, "Oh, you're real, you're real! Oh, Aslan!" She and Susan both then "covered him with kisses." Lucy's response is particularly interesting in light of Jesus' promises of the coming Spirit in John 14. Jesus tells his disciples "On that day you will realize that I am in my Father, and you are in me, and I am in you" (20). What Jesus promises to his disciples is a realization—we might say a deeper knowledge—of who Jesus is: of both the indwelling relation of the Son to the Father, and the intimate indwelling of God in his people, and God's people in him. Lucy's exclamation gets at that, doesn't it—albeit somewhat simply? "Oh, you're real, you're real!" This is a movement from doubt to faith: an expression of belief not just in an idea, but in a person. Lucy has come to a deeper realization of the presence and reality of Aslan.

Lucy and Susan then cover Aslan with kisses, which is a beautiful and childlike expression of love. There is a certain extravagance to it, and Aslan accepts that expression. So much of Jesus' teaching about the Holy Spirit in John 14 is about love: the love for Jesus of those who follow him, the love of the Father for those who follow Jesus. Love is mentioned seven times. The promise of the Holy Spirit is also a promise of Jesus' own presence with his followers. In a mysterious way, the presence of the Third Person of the Trinity in the lives of those who obey God is the presence of the fullness of God (Father, Son, and Holy Spirit) in us. Jesus gets at that in multiple ways in John 14. For example, he tells his followers, "Anyone who loves me will obey my teaching. My Father will love them, and we will come to them and make our home with them" (23). Note the important use of the first-person plural pronoun "we." Jesus speaks not only of sending the Holy Spirit to dwell in us, but through the Spirit he says "we will come to them"—the "we" including both himself and the Father." Again later he says, "I am going away and I am coming back to you" (28). How is he coming back to his followers? Through the Holy Spirit.

Consider again the phrase in the passage above where Aslan's breath comes upon Susan: "a rich sort of smell that seemed to hang about his hair came all over her." Something in the very presence of Aslan himself, something that hangs about him—something Susan identifies (or which we might say Lewis symbolizes) through a rich sort of smell—comes upon Susan with Aslan's breath. The Holy Spirit that comes in the breath of Aslan is the presence of Aslan himself. Again, there is great mystery here, and my goal isn't to try to unravel it all, or to try to make a mathematical formula of it, but rather to see how such biblical language may have inspired C.S. Lewis's writing of his Narnia stories, and perhaps how those stories might imaginatively help us to better understand or appreciate the presence and work of the Spirit in and with us.

AN ANOINTING KISS

Two more aspects of this passage are worth noting with respect to the imagery of the Holy Spirit in Aslan's breath. The first is the kiss that Aslan gives to Susan on her forehead. Here, in the first of his Narnia stories, Lewis describes it as a lick on the forehead. Yet we often describe the lick of a cat or dog as a kiss, and indeed in later books Lewis will use a different verb, writing of Aslan kissing the foreheads of characters. This symbolism suggests a sort of anointing. Anointing is an important rite or sacrament in Scripture. It is a setting aside of somebody (or something) for a holy purpose. Traditionally, a person is anointed with oil on the head (Leviticus 8:12; Exodus 29:7; Psalm 23:5; Luke 7:46), which is where Aslan kisses Susan. In relation to the symbolism of breath and spirit, though, the most important aspect of these passages is that an anointing often precedes or is associated with one being filled with the Holy Spirit.

Consider Acts 10:38 in which Peter describes the anointing of Jesus "with the Holy Spirit and power." Jesus himself references this anointing in Luke 4:18–19 when he quotes from the start of Isaiah 61.

> The Spirit of the Lord is on me,
> because he has anointed me
> to proclaim good news to the poor.
> He has sent me to proclaim freedom for the prisoners
> and recovery of sight for the blind,

to set the oppressed free,
to proclaim the year of the Lord's favor.

Anointing is again associated with the powerful presence of the Holy Spirit.
Although in this passage Jesus speaks as the one who fulfills that prophecy—and thus as the one who has been anointed rather than the one doing
the anointing—the anointing of others by God or in God's name is important
symbolism in Scripture. We see this in Paul's words to the Corinthian church
(2 Corinthians 1:21–22): "Now it is God who makes both us and you stand firm
in Christ. He anointed us, set his seal of ownership on us, and put his Spirit in
our hearts as a deposit, guaranteeing what is to come." When Samuel anointed
Saul as king (1 Samuel 10:1), he did so with both oil and a kiss. He also said to
Saul, "the Spirit of the Lord will come powerfully upon you" (1 Samuel 10:6).

We read of the same thing with Samuel's anointing of David: "So Samuel
took the horn of oil and anointed him in the presence of his brothers, and from
that day on the Spirit of the LORD came powerfully upon David" (1 Samuel
16:13). Paul also wrote of laying hands on Timothy (a physical touch rather than
the pouring of oil[3]), and of imparting to him through that action a spiritual gift:
"For this reason I remind you to fan into flame the gift of God, which is in you
through the laying on of my hands. For the Spirit God gave us does not make us
timid, but gives us power, love and self-discipline" (2 Timothy 1:6–7). This laying
on of hands is also a sort of anointing and blessing, and we read in the same
passage that Paul also references the gift of the Holy Spirit and the power and
love that comes from the Spirit. An anointing is followed by the coming of the
Holy Spirit. So, too, with the possibility of the lick being a sort of anointing: it is
followed by Aslan's breath.

If this was the only reference to Aslan's tongue on the forehead of one of
his followers, and if it was not connected to a symbol of the Holy Spirit, I might
be hesitant to see in it a symbol of anointing. I might think of little more than
a large, warm, moist tongue as a symbol of affection—and perhaps an appeal
to the imagination of a young reader who might find both a terror and a thrill

---

3   It seems likely to me, given the cultural associations of anointing, that Paul also would have poured
    oil on Timothy, but if so it is not mentioned in the text—only the laying on of hands.

at the thought of being licked by a lion. But it is not the only reference. In later books, Lewis will write of the lion's tongue on a forehead as a "kiss" and not a "lick," and it will again be connected with other images related to anointing. We will return to this in later chapters, but we now leave this passage with a final note: both a promise and a command of Jesus to his followers related to the coming of the Holy Spirit.

Above we considered the John 20:21–22 passage which describes Jesus, through the action of his breath upon his disciples, giving both the gift of peace and the promise of the Holy Spirit. This was not the first time he gave the promise of peace associated with the Holy Spirit. In an earlier discourse recorded in John 14:25–27, Jesus also promised the coming of "the Advocate, the Holy Spirit" whom the Father will send in his name. He then said, "Peace I leave with you; My peace I give you.... Do not let your hearts be troubled and do not be afraid." Through his Holy Spirit, God grants peace. Because of the Spirit, our hearts do not need to be troubled or fearful.

This, too, we see reflected in the scene at the Stone Table. It is yet another connection between Aslan's breath and the Holy Spirit. Prior to Aslan's breath coming over Susan, we read that the girls were both miserable and fearful. Even after Aslan appears, both girls remain "almost as much frightened as they were glad." After Aslan breathes on Susan (and perhaps on Lucy also, though the text emphasizes his breath on Susan) there is no more mention of fear. First, the two girls become calmer. And then we see them joyful and even playful. They have "such a romp as no one has ever had except in Narnia." Imagine being tossed in the air but a giant lion. Even then, they felt no fear. Whether intentional or not, it is a lovely portrayal of what we would expect of the Holy Spirit's work in the lives of the two girls—and of how the Holy Spirit can work in our lives, too, if we let him.

THE HOLY SPIRIT AND THE SYMBOLISM OF FLAME

The resurrection scene at the Stone Table is the first reference in the Chronicles of Narnia to Aslan's breath. Perhaps this symbolism seeming to point to the Holy Spirit was unintentional. Perhaps it came instinctively and

subconsciously from the mind of the author, stem-
ming from more than two decades of walking with
the Lord and pondering Scripture, and of the
understanding of the Holy Spirit that would
have grown in him over that time. Or perhaps
it flowed from his knowledge of Greek. Whether
the imagery was initially intentional or not is not
important. The references to Aslan's breath recur
several more times, often in connec-
tion with a kiss, and the narrative also
connects Aslan's breath to other biblical
symbols of the Holy Spirit, including (as we
will soon see) flames.

The second reference to Aslan's breath in *The
Lion, the Witch and the Wardrobe* comes in the next
chapter (Chapter 16) when Aslan goes to the
castle of the White Witch and brings the
stone statues back to life. It is a longer passage beginning almost as soon as Aslan
leaps over the walls into the Witch's
castle. "He had bounded up to the
stone lion and breathed on him.
Then without waiting a moment
he whisked round—almost as if he
had been a cat chasing its tail—
and breathed also on the stone
dwarf." Aslan moves quickly
from the dwarf to a Dryad, then
a rabbit, and then a pair of centaurs.
The narrative then brings our attention
back to the stone lion.

I expect you've seen someone put a lighted match to a bit of newspaper which is propped up in a grate against an unlit fire. And for a second nothing seems to have happened; and then you notice a tiny streak of flame creeping along the edge of the newspaper. It was like that now. For a second after Aslan had breathed upon him the stone lion looked just the same. Then a tiny streak of gold began to run along his white marble back—then it spread—then the colour seemed to lick all over him as the flame licks all over a bit of paper—then, while his hindquarters were still obviously stone the lion shook his mane and all the heavy, stony fold rippled in living hair.

The full scene makes four mentions of Aslan breathing on something—or, rather, on some*one* since the object of his breath in each case is a stone statue that was once (and will once again be) a creature from Narnia. Unlike the passage above that speaks of Aslan's breath as a noun, all four of these references use *breathe* as a verb. Aslan is the one who breathes. This may bring to mind the active verb in John 20:21–22 when Jesus breathed on his disciples.

Note the fire imagery describing the change that comes over the stone lion as it transforms back to living flesh. Though Jesus sometimes uses fire (including unquenchable fire) as a symbol of judgement (for example, Luke 3:17, John 15:6, etc.), John the Baptist (in the Gospel accounts of Matthew and Luke), Paul (in 2 Timothy), and Luke (in the book of Acts) all use fire imagery to reveal the baptism or presence of the Holy Spirit. Acts 2:1–4 is an excellent starting point. Describing the disciples shortly after Jesus' ascension, Luke tells us:

> When the day of Pentecost came, they were all together in one place. Suddenly a sound like the blowing of a violent wind came from heaven and filled the whole house where they were sitting. They saw what seemed to be tongues of fire that separated and came to rest on each of them. All of them were filled with the Holy Spirit and began to speak in other tongues as the Spirit enabled them. (Acts 2:1–4)

We have referenced Pentecost already. Jewish Pentecost (or *Shavuot*) was a celebration of God's giving the Torah to Moses at Mount Sinai. Like many Jewish festivals and celebrations (especially the Passover), Pentecost became meaningful in a new way to those Jews who became followers of Christ (and later to all Christians) as the day the Holy Spirit came in power: the day that Jesus' promise of the Holy Spirit was fulfilled. The coming of the Holy Spirit is an important moment, made manifest to the crowds not only by the disciples speaking in other languages, but also by visible flames—or at least what *appeared* to be tongues of fire—coming to rest on the disciples.

This is not the only time the Scriptures use flame or fire imagery to describe the presence of the Holy Spirit. We read in Matthew 3:11 that John the Baptist told the crowds, "I baptize you with water for repentance. But after me comes one who is more powerful than I, whose sandals I am not worthy to carry. He will baptize you with the Holy Spirit and fire." (See also Luke 3:16.) Though the wording allows us to interpret the "Holy Spirit and fire" as two separate baptisms, or perhaps two separate aspects of the same baptism, the important point is that the coming of the Holy Spirit is associated with this imagery of fire. In the 2 Timothy 1:6 passage cited above, Paul wrote to Timothy of "fan[ning] into flame the gift of God." Although the connection of the flame imagery is not quite as tightly connected to the Holy Spirit in this passage, it is there in the metaphor of fanning a flame. Whatever this gift of Timothy is, it is not a *natural* talent; Paul describes it as a gift *of God,* which is to say a spiritual gift: something given to him by and through the Holy Spirit, who is indeed mentioned in the next verse.

Lewis used similar language and visual imagery to describe the appearance of the stone statues. They weren't actual flames licking the stone lion, but the appearance is *like* flames that creep along the edge of a newspaper. A paragraph later, the narrative references the scene with more fire imagery, noting "the courtyard was now a blaze of colours." Once we pay attention to the connection between breath and the Holy Spirit in biblical language (and languages), as well as in the John 20 passage describing Jesus breathing on his disciples and imparting to them the gift of the Holy Spirit, and we begin to pay attention to Lewis's language of the breath of Aslan, additional connections to the Holy Spirit begin to pop out.

It is not merely or even primarily a literary interest in Lewis's use of breath and anointing that is of interest to me—observations I cannot claim to be original even if I personally had not seen them before. My deeper interest is in how Lewis's insights shed light on a biblical understanding of the person of the Holy Spirit and the Spirit's transformative power in our lives.

THE SPIRIT GIVES LIFE, TRANSFORMS, AND RENEWS

We need look no farther than the passage of the stone statues to see some of these further connections and insights into spiritual transformation. Consider the following biblical teachings—from both Jesus and Paul—about the Holy Spirit. John's Gospel records Jesus saying the following: "The Spirit gives life; the flesh counts for nothing. The words I have spoken to you—they are full of the Spirit and life" (John 6:63). In his letter to the Romans, Paul wrote, "because through Christ Jesus the law of the Spirit who gives life has set you free from the law of sin and death" (8:2). And a little later in the letter he added, "But if Christ is in you, then even though your body is subject to death because of sin, the Spirit gives life because of righteousness" (8:10).

The Spirit gives life. Along with Paul's teaching earlier in Romans that it is through the Holy Spirit that God pours love into our hearts (5:5), this truth that the Holy Spirit gives life may be the most important thing we can learn about the Spirit. And this is precisely what we see happening—in a very visual and visceral way—in the scene at the witch's castle. Prior to Aslan breathing on them, these stone statues have no life. They are breathless. Cold. Still. Dead. The narrator tells us the scene had been "deadly white" and filled with "deadly silence." When Aslan breathes on the creatures, they stir to life. "Everywhere the statues were coming to life.... The whole place rang with the sound of happy roarings, brayings, yelpings, barkings, squealings, cooings, neighings, stampings, shouts, hurrahs, songs and laughter." The spirit gives life. Aslan's breath gives life.

There is yet another language we could use to describe this scene, and it would also fit the biblical teaching on the Holy Spirit. Still later in Romans, Paul writes, "Do not conform to the pattern of this world, but be transformed by the renewing of your mind. Then you will be able to test and approve what God's will is—his good, pleasing and perfect will" (12:2). There are two words in this passage of particular relevance, translated into English as "transformed" and "renewing." Which is to say, Paul was writing about spiritual transformation and renewal. There is also something very interesting in Paul's use of the verb "transformed": it is in the passive voice, meaning Paul's readers are acted upon

rather than the ones doing the acting. Yet
Paul's words are also a command.
Paul did not write to the Roman
Christians telling them to transform themselves. He told them
to be *transformed*. That means
transformation is something
done to them (and to us), or
in them (and in us); we are the
objects of transformation, not the
primary actors. And
yet the fact that it is
a command means it
requires our obedience and participation. Who is the actor who does the
work of transformation and renewal?
It is God who transforms and renews

us. Specifically, it is the Holy Spirit. This is one
reason it is appropriate for Christians to speak of *spiritual* transformation and
spiritual renewal: it involves both our spirits and the Holy Spirit.[4]

This is not the only place Paul used such language of spiritual renewal.
In Ephesians 4:22–23, he wrote, "You were taught ... to be made new in the
attitude of your minds." Here, too, we see a similar grammatical structure
putting a teaching into the passive voice, indicating that it is God who does the
transforming and renewing work through his Spirit living in us, and yet we
are called to participate in the renewal. And again in 2 Corinthians 3:17–18,

4   Much more could be written about spiritual transformation and this mystery captured by a
    command given in the passive voice: that our spiritual transformation is God's work in us and
    yet we are called to participate in that work. Readers may wonder how we do that. How do
    we actively allow God's work in us, while recognizing it is God's work? This is a vitally important
    question, and in the view of the author any encouragement this book gives to take part in that
    transformation is the most important thing it could accomplish. The topic is also far beyond the
    scope of this book. Readers are encouraged to explore some of the classic works on spiritual
    disciplines, such as Richard Foster's *Celebration of Discipline,* or to explore the resources of
    Renovare at renovare.org. I have explored this in one of my earlier books, *Disciple Making in
    a Culture of Power, Comfort, and Fear.*

the language of transformation—this time with explicit reference to the Spirit of the Lord: "Now the Lord is the Spirit, and where the Spirit of the Lord is, there is freedom. And we all, who with unveiled faces contemplate the Lord's glory, are being transformed into his image with ever-increasing glory, which comes from the Lord, who is the Spirit." We do not transform ourselves. Yet we are transformed. It is God's work in us. And that transformational work in us brings freedom.

What we see in the scene at the castle of the White Witch can be described, as we noted early, as the breath of Aslan bringing life. But we might also see this as a moment of transformation. And, given that all the stone statues were prisoners of the White Witch, the transformation also brought freedom. The bodies are being transformed from stone to living flesh. In a very real sense, they are being renewed, and then freed from captivity. Even while stone, they were still bodies in the shapes of the creatures. So Aslan is not creating something brand new here. Rather, he is breathing on something that already exists and transforming it to something new: taking something that once had life but has turned to stone, and renewing the life within it.

It is also interesting to note, in light of 2 Corinthians 3:17–18, that the first creature Aslan renews is another lion. All the creatures of Narnia are, in some way, the image-bearers of their creator. But in terms of the symbolism of spiritual transformation, the lion is especially transformed into Aslan's image. I think it is an important spiritual message that Aslan chose a lion to be the first creature transformed. We could write many books just on the biblical principles of spiritual renewal and transformation, apart from our exploration of the Narnia stories. God desires to transform and renew his people. His people should desire that transformation. Yet we cannot accomplish this by our own effort. We cannot transform ourselves any more than we can bring about our own salvation, any more than the stone statues could transform themselves back to flesh. It took the breath of Aslan. The power of Aslan.

If there is one important thing in the Narnia passage that is different from the biblical passages about transformation, it is that obedience does not seem required of those being transformed from stone back to life. They did not follow any command or make any choice to allow themselves to "be transformed." No exhortation was needed. Yet it is clear from their responses afterward that all of them were eager to obey Aslan. And indeed, the very reason they had been turned to stone was most likely their refusal to obey the White Witch.

Aslan's breath, like the Holy Spirit, is a free gift. His breath transforms and renews. That gift brings life and freedom. And the joyous scenes both of the resurrection of Aslan and the giving of his breath at the Stone Table and then of the resurrection of Aslan's followers and the giving of his breath in the courtyard show that the transformation and renewal is something we can accept with joy.

II

PRINCE CASPIAN: RETURN TO NARNIA

Growing Bigger

There was a time when *Prince Caspian* was my least favorite of the Narnia books. I remember somebody describing it as the most martial of the seven volumes: the one most focused on military actions. Although this is a more accurate description of the 2008 film adaptation than of the book itself, it still holds some truth. Most of the story takes place in the context of a war for control of Narnia: a cross between an armed rebellion against an occupying army (which never really gets off the ground) and a tyrannical conqueror seeking to crush the already-conquered (a much more likely outcome apart from divine intervention). Although some of the other books (*The Lion, the Witch and the Wardrobe, The Horse and His Boy,* and *The Last Battle*) have short battle scenes, nearly all of *Prince Caspian* takes place in the context of a war, with descriptions of battles, military strategies, and casualties.

When I reread the book, however, I am quickly captivated. And the complaint about the militarism seems at least in part to be an unjust criticism. Although Lewis devoted quite a few words to the duel between the Narnian High King Peter and the Telmarine usurper-king Miraz, fewer words are given to describing the military actions between the Old Narnians and the Telmarines. As Trumpkin recounts for the four Pevensies the events that led to his trip to the ruins of Cair Paravel on the peninsula-turned-island, his focus is much more on the thoughts, feelings, and worries of the characters involved, and on interpersonal conflicts between them, than on details of the fighting. Readers get only a summary of what the war has been like, often with whole days compressed into single sentences. It is not unlike J.R.R. Tolkien's telling of the Battle of Five Armies in *The Hobbit*—a major battle to be sure, but Bilbo, our witness to the events, gets knocked unconscious early on, so readers get only a few paragraphs describing the battle, mostly told after it has ended. Criticism that *The Hobbit* centers on (and glorifies) violence may be an accurate description of Peter Jackson's films, but not of the books themselves. Tolkien does much the same thing with the Siege of Minas Tirith in *The Lord of the Rings*, putting the focus not on the bloody details of the battlefield, but on the experience of Pippin watching from the walls. One of the few scenes where readers find themselves down on the battlefield is the personal confrontation between Éowyn and the Witch-King. This is also Lewis's approach in *Prince Caspian*. Rather than focusing on the battle scenes, the themes of the story center more on what it means to believe something that nobody else believes, what it means to follow Aslan when following him is difficult and risky and unpopular, where and how we seek power, and the sort of spiritual awakening that moves a people from slavery to freedom.

As in *The Lion, the Witch and the Wardrobe*, much of the narrative in *Prince Caspian* involving the Pevensies just recounts them walking through the woods of Narnia—except they gain the dwarf Trumpkin as their companion rather than Mr. and Mrs. Beaver. The journey involves some beautiful moments, including a scene evoking a sense of *sehnsucht* when Lucy has her middle-of-the-night wandering and senses the Dryads on the verge of waking. Some of these scenes strike me as descriptions of how the Holy Spirit moves in the hearts of seekers with a sense of longing, which is not unlike how Lewis described his own spiritual journey from atheism to Christian faith. As noted above, Lucy's experience also contains spiritual lessons about what it means to trust and follow God even when nobody around you is doing so.

Although *Prince Caspian* contains many passages that can be read as spiritual journeys in which the Holy Spirit is at work, there are only four passages that specifically reference Aslan's breath. The first comes in Chapter 10, "The Return of the Lion." As with the first reference to Aslan's breath in *The Lion, the Witch and the Wardrobe*, it begins with an anointing of Lucy, though this time described neither as a lick or a kiss, but merely the light touch of his tongue, on her nose rather than her forehead.

> The great beast rolled over on his side so that Lucy fell, half sitting and half lying between his front paws. He bent forward and just touched her nose with his tongue. His warm breath came all round her. She gazed up into the large wise face.
>
> "Welcome child," he said.
>
> "Aslan," said Lucy, "you're bigger."
>
> "That is because you are older, little one," answered he.
>
> "Not because you are?"
>
> "I am not. But every year you grow, you will find me bigger."

The dialogue continues for a time, as Aslan gently explains to Lucy the nature of the task ahead of her. Lucy is not excited about this task. It will involve her following Aslan whether the others come with her or not. And Aslan makes it clear they will not even see him at first and might not believe Lucy, who already knows from her experiences at the start of *The Lion, the Witch and the Wardrobe* what a difficult thing it is not to be believed. Who can blame her for not wanting to return to that situation? She is understandably distraught. She wants Aslan to just "come roaring in and frighten the enemy away." Instead, Lucy is called to step outside her comfort zone, and beyond any promise of safety or success. Upon hearing this, "Lucy buried her head in his mane to hide from his face. But there must have been magic in his mane. She could feel lion-strength going into her. Quite suddenly, she sat up." And then she says, very simply, "I'm sorry, Aslan. I'm ready now."

THE SYMBOLISM AND USES OF MAGIC

One of the starting points in understanding this passage (and its relevance to a portrayal of the Holy Spirit) is Lewis's use of the word *magic*. For many Christians, any reference to magic (other than one of condemnation) is troublesome, and so it's important to see just what Lewis is, and is not, doing with this imagery.

In common usage, magic refers to something that does not follow the laws of physics or normal natural processes. That is, magic is something *super*natural rather than merely natural. Magic stands in contrast with the material world and its physical laws. In that sense, the concept of *magic* shares something in common with the concept of *spiritual.* And that's an important hint. The reference to "magic in his mane" should cue readers that there is something supernatural or spiritual about Aslan's mane that Lucy buries herself in at the end of the scene. Since this scene begins with Aslan breathing on Lucy—with his breath coming "all around her" much the way the scent of his mane does when her face is buried in it—the word "magic" seems to apply to the impact of his breath as well as his mane. Sometimes a sword really is just a sword, but the word "magic" hints that Aslan's breath and his mane *are* more than just warm air and fur.

To deepen our understanding—and dispel concerns that Lewis's use of the word "magic" somehow promotes witchcraft or the occult—it is helpful to look at the writings of both C.S. Lewis and his friend and fellow author of fantasy literature J.R.R. Tolkien to see how they portrayed magic in their fictional works and also what they had to say about it in nonfiction writings. Fortunately, both authors wrote about this topic on multiple occasions. Although they had a few subtle differences in their use of magic as a literary device, they shared some important ideas and seemed to have had an influence upon each other.

Both authors frequently used magic in their fictional worlds as a literary device to represent technology and especially technological power, which Lewis also referred to as "applied science." Think of anything from a digital computer to an automobile to a refrigerator or microwave oven. Few of us have a deep understanding of how these work, and fewer of us could construct one. Although I take them for granted and intellectually understand that they operate based on material laws of physics and chemistry, they are mysterious to me. Like magic, these technological devices take difficult tasks and make them effortless for me. I put my leftover coffee in the refrigerator on a hot summer day, and a few hours later it has turned cold.

Of course, I don't believe that my refrigerator, microwave oven, or Subaru Outback is magic; I know they work on scientific principles. Yet because technology is so often both mysterious and powerful, literary magic functions as a good symbol for it. In a famous letter to a potential publisher (published in *The Letters of J. R. R. Tolkien*), Tolkien describes some of the major themes in *The Lord of the Rings.* He explicitly connects "Machine" and "Magic," stating "By [Magic] I intend all use of external plans or devices (apparatus) instead of development of inner powers or talents—or even the use of these talents with the corrupted motive of dominating: bulldozing the real world, or coercing other wills." He goes on to add, "The Machine is our more obvious modern form though more closely related to Magic than is usually recognized" (185).

In *The Abolition of Man,* Lewis associated some uses of magic with applied science and with "technique," a word that shares that same root as technology. There are numerous times in the Narnia stories that some sort of magical power is referenced with negative or evil connotations. These include the White Witch's use of magic to ensure it remains always winter in Narnia and to turn creatures into stone. The Emerald Witch in *The Silver Chair* and her casting of a spell on Prince Rilian to enslave him certainly falls in the same category. Aslan describes this sort of magic as "dark magic," noting at the end of *The Magician's Nephew* that Jadis "has fled far away into the North of the world; she will live on there, growing stronger in dark Magic" (Chapter 14). The best example of Lewis's connection of magic and modern technology (and the evil associations of the use of magic to gain power over others) might be the eponymous "magician" of that same story whose description—especially his lab coat and his experimentation with guinea pigs—seems much more like that of an evil scientist than a wizard.

It would be wrong, however, to suggest that Lewis always associated magic with evil, or that he only used magic to portray technology. Both Tolkien and Lewis also portrayed magic in their literary works as a device to create art. Indeed, magic can be symbolic of the artistic endeavor itself. To say that art and story are capable of enchanting us, of casting a spell over us, connects us to the etymological roots of story. In Old English, the word *spel* meant a story. The word *gospel* comes from Old English *god spel* meaning "good story." *God spel* was the translation of the Latin *evangelium* into the language of the English people. That same word *spel* that meant "story" also came to mean a "spell" in the sense of an enchantment or incantation. In the same letter quoted above, Tolkien wrote of the Elves that "[t]heir 'magic' is Art, delivered from many of its human limitations: more effortless, more quick, more complete ... and its object is Art not Power, sub- creation not domination" (186).

There is yet a third way that both Lewis and Tolkien seemed to use magic as a literary device. It has been noted that figures like Tolkien's wizard Gandalf or Lewis's magician Coriakin both bear resemblance to great Hebrew prophets Elijah, Elisha, and Moses, whose many miracles would have appeared as magic to those who saw them. We can even see some analogy of certain types of magic in the Narnia stories to the Christian notion of the gifts of the Spirit. Healing and prophecy, for example, are very much at home in fantasy settings such as Narnia. These are not natural or physical abilities, nor can they be described as talents developed through practice; rather, they are spiritual and supernatural gifts.

In any case, there are numerous examples of magic in the Narnia stories that are associated with the Good. In Chapter 10 of *The Voyage of the Dawn Treader,* Coriakin is described as ruling the island of the Dufflepuds by "rough magic," and is approved by Aslan for doing so. Very much like a wizard (and perhaps a little like Moses) he walks around with "a curiously carved staff." He also has a book of spells called *"the* Book, the Magic Book." In the same story, Old Man Ramandu and his daughter live on an island of enchantment in which the meals at Aslan's Table are magically renewed every day. Father Christmas also has a powerful magic that we see in *The Lion, the Witch and the Wardrobe.* These are only a few examples, and *Prince Caspian* is no exception. The half-dwarf Cornelius is capable of some small feats of magic. We see many magical beasts and creatures including the Greek demigods Bacchus and Silenus who magically provide a wonderful feast and tear down the bridge of the evil Narnians. But most important example is the magic of Aslan—including the Deeper Magic from before the Dawn of Time.

TWO TYPES OF MAGIC

What makes this even more complex is that there are not only different uses of magic as a literary device, but also multiple types of magic. Or perhaps more accurately we might say there are multiple different concepts or sources of supernatural power that are often described with the single English word *magic*. In a dialogue between Galadriel and Sam Gamgee in *The Lord of the Rings*, J.R.R. Tolkien illustrates this through the wise character Galadriel, who points out that there are two very different concepts of power, both of which are described by the single word *magic*: "For this is what your folk would call magic, I believe; though I do not understand clearly what they mean; and they seem to use the same word of the deceits of the Enemy. But this, if you will, is the magic of Galadriel" (II/7).

Similarly, Lewis wrote about (at least) two types of supernatural or spiritual powers which he distinguishes by using two different Greek words *goeteia* and *magia* ascribing to them different variations of meaning even though both are (unfortunately) often translated into the single English word *magic*. *Goeteia* is generally associated with witchcraft, sorcery, or

necromancy, and often works through the conjuring of spirits whose power is then controlled or manipulated by the conjuring magician. We see this *goeteia* magic in the iconic example of the genie in the lamp; whoever controls the lamp controls the power of the genie. *Goeteia* is also at work in the seances and rites portrayed in literature and film (and also believed by some to be at work in the real world) to conjure up spirits for various purposes. This also seems to be the sort of "magic" employed by the medium whom Saul consults in 1 Samuel 28:3–25 to raise the spirit of Samuel. And again, the use of a spirit to gain power or make a profit is also involved in the story of the slave girl whom Paul heals of demon possession (Acts 16:16–34)—much to the chagrin of her owners, who can no longer profit from her powers. At its core, *goeteia* (whether achieved through conjuring spirits or otherwise) is about gaining power, and in particular gaining power over others. It is an oppressive and destructive power, both in its means and in its ends.

Not surprisingly, both Lewis and Tolkien portrayed this sort of magic as evil, and they especially associated it with technological power, and used it as a symbol in that way. In his short but important book *The Abolition of Man,* Lewis wrote:

> There is something which unites magic and applied science while separating both from the "wisdom" of earlier ages.... For magic and applied science alike the problem is how to subdue reality to the wishes of men: the solution is a technique; and both, in the practice of this technique, are ready to do things hitherto regarded as disgusting and impious. (83–84)

This view is reflected in the *goeteia* magic that the dwarf Nikabrik and his friends seek to use in *Prince Caspian* to bring back the White Witch from the dead, so that they can use her power to overthrow Miraz. The scene where this plays out is in a chapter tellingly titled "Sorcery and Sudden Vengeance" (Chapter 12). The very unsympathetic character Nikabrik voices the precise thing that Lewis associated with *goeteia* and which both Lewis and Tolkien used as a symbol for technology. "We want power," Nikabrik says, "and we want a power that will be on our side." Caspian gives this plan a name and description: "Black sorcery and the calling up of an accursed spirit."

In the opening chapter of *The Silver Chair*, Eustace also contemplates attempting some sort of ritualistic magic to get into Narnia: drawing a circle on the ground, writing strange letters or symbols in it, standing inside the circle, and reciting charms and spells. Yet he quickly (and correctly) realizes it would be wrong. "That was the sort of thing I was thinking of, though I never did it. But now that it comes to the point, I've an idea that all those circles and things are rather rot. I don't think [Aslan would] like them. It would look as if we thought we could make him do things."

There is, however, another concept often also associated with the English word magic, which Lewis connects with the Greek word *magia* to clearly distinguish it from *goeteia*. In *That Hideous Strength*, Lewis's Arthurian fantasy novel set in modern-day England—the third and final book of his Ransom trilogy published six years before *Prince Caspian*—Cecil Dimble addresses these two concepts of magic.

> For [Merlin] every operation on Nature is a kind of personal contact, like coaxing a child or stroking one's horse. After him came the modern man to whom Nature is something dead—a machine to be worked, and taken to bits if it won't work the way he pleases. Finally, come the Belbury people, who take over that view from the modern man unaltered and simply want to increase their power by tacking on to it the aid of spirits—extra-natural, anti-natural spirits . . . They thought the old *magia* of Merlin, which worked in with the spiritual qualities of Nature, loving and reverencing them and knowing them from within, could be combined with the new *goeteia*—the brutal surgery from without. . . . In a sense Merlin represents what we've got to get back to in some different way. (134)

Consider some of the important differences between the *magia* of Merlin and the *goeteia* of the story's villains (the "Belbury people," also known as the NICE) that come out in this passage. *Goeteia* is described as a "brutal surgery" and its purpose is power. The villains, seeking to increase their power, want to employ *goeteia* in addition to their technological and political power. But it turns out Merlin won't be used that way. His *magia* works in a different way and with different purposes. It works through the "*spiritual* qualities of Nature, loving and reverencing them and knowing them from within" [emphasis added]. This is important. The wise character Dimble describes this type of *magia* magic not merely as supernatural but as *spiritual.* In Merlin's case, it relates to the spiritual qualities of nature. When I hear that phrase, I think of Psalm 148 which describes the sun, moon, stars, waters, sea creatures, mountains, fruit trees, cedars, wild animals, cattle, small creatures, and birds—a rather extensive list of aspects of nature and the created world—all taking part in the spiritual act of worship.

Even Empress Jadis from Charn (also known as the White Witch) recognizes the difference between the two types of magic. In Chapter 8 of *The Magician's Nephew,* as she observes Aslan's creative power singing Narnia into existence and then filling it with light and life, the narrator notes, "Ever since the song began she had felt that this whole world was filled with a Magic different from hers and stronger. She hated it. She would have smashed that whole world, or all worlds, to pieces, if it would only stop the singing." These two types of power—that of Jadis and that of Aslan, both of which are referred to as magic—are so fundamentally different that a being who practices one could find the other hateful.

And this brings us back to the sort of magic that Lucy senses in and around Aslan after he breaths on her. While the "spiritual" quality of Merlin's magic comes from nature, the spiritual quality of Aslan's magic comes from Aslan himself. This breath of Aslan is, indeed, of the Spirit: the breath or spirit of Aslan himself: the *ruach elohim.*

ASLAN LOOKS BIGGER. LUCY IS BIGGER. AND SO IS EDMUND.

And this brings us back to the impact of Aslan's breath on Lucy. And on us. In the imagery the breath of Aslan, the Narnia stories offer profound glimpses of the Holy Spirit and his work in our lives.

Lewis's insights are many—here in this passage, and in the passages to come. One particularly evident element in this passage is the explicit reference to growth. Lucy is bigger. And as Aslan says to her, "Every year you grow, you will find me bigger." To understand Lewis's use of the word "bigger", which seems to be a description of spiritual rather than physical grown, it is helpful to briefly skip ahead to Chapter 8 and the third reference to Aslan's breath in *Prince Caspian* where we find similar language. The passage describes Edmund when he appears before Lord Glozelle and Lord Sopespian in order to challenge Miraz to a duel with Peter. The narrator describes Edmund from the perspective of these two Telmarines. "Between [the Centaur and the Giant / Wimbleweather stood] a figure they could not recognize. Nor indeed would the other boys at Edmund's school have recognized him if they could have seen him at that moment. For Aslan had breathed on him at their meeting and a kind of greatness hung about him." Unlike with Lucy in the previous passage, here the reader is explicitly told that Edmund's greatness is a result of Aslan's breathing on him. That's an important connection. Greatness is another word for bigness. Sometimes "great" simply means physically large, though it more often means bigness of another kind. What kind of greatness hangs about Edmund? The passage doesn't say explicitly, but it doesn't seem to be anything the narrator can pinpoint with *physical* characteristics. Edmund isn't any taller or heavier or more muscular. At least not that we are told. But he is *greater*. If it isn't a definable physical characteristic, it might be fair to describe it as something more than physical. Which is to say, as something spiritual. Whatever it is, it is notable that this greatness is palpable even in the midst of his enemies.

When I read this passage about Edmund standing before his enemies (and the enemies of Narnia), I think of Stephen (the first martyr) when he comes before the Sanhedrin in the long passage beginning in Acts 6:5 and running through Acts 7. This passage begins by noting that Stephen was "full of faith and of the Holy Spirit." That is the context for all that follows; the Holy Spirit was working in Stephen. What was the result of that work? Shortly after this reference to Stephen being filled with the Spirit, Luke described him as "a man full of God's grace and power" (6:8). And then we read that those who tried to argue with him "could not stand up against the wisdom the Spirit gave him as he spoke" (6:10). Finally, when he comes before the Sanhedrin to stand trial before his enemies, Luke's account tells us, "they saw that his face was like the face of an angel" (6:15). Note three times in these four verses Acts explicitly attributes elements of Stephen's greatness—the fullness of his faith, his power, and his wisdom—to the Holy Spirit. These are examples of spiritual growth or greatness in Stephen.

I'm not sure how any of the Sanhedrin knew what an angel was like. There doesn't seem to be any purely physical description that would capture the scene. But we do understand an angel to be a spiritual being. I'd venture to say that both as he carried out the work of God, and then as he stood before his enemies, a kind of spiritual greatness hung over Stephen *as a result of the presence of the Holy Spirit,* even as a sort of greatness hung over Edmund *as result of Aslan's breath upon him.* Edmund is bigger.

Lucy is also bigger. It is unlikely that she has suddenly grown taller because of Aslan's breath upon her moments earlier. One year has passed (in her own world) since she last encountered Aslan, so she has probably grown a little bit physically in that time (before Aslan breathed on her in this scene). But it is only after Aslan breathes on Lucy that we read any reference to her being bigger; it is also only after Aslan breathes on her that Aslan himself looked bigger to her. Her recognition of his bigness, we are told, came as result of her own growth. Like Edmund, Lucy is bigger in some way. And Lewis has tied that to the breath of Aslan.

Much of the New Testament—at some level, we might say *all* of it, and indeed all of Scripture—is given to us that we might know God more fully, and as we know him that we might also grow closer to him, and in our faith in him, and in our likeness of him, and in our obedience to him. In Ephesians 4:11–16, Paul uses the metaphor of a physical body maturing from infancy to adulthood to illustrate spiritual growth. As we grow in knowledge of Christ, "we will no longer be infants, tossed back and forth by the waves, and blown here and there by every wind of teaching and by the cunning and craftiness of people in their deceitful scheming. Instead, speaking the truth in love, we will grow to become in every respect the mature body of him who is the head, that is, Christ." There is far too much in this passage to unravel here. For one thing, though some of the language suggests the spiritual maturing of the individual Christian, the context of the passage is the maturing of the church body as a whole. The spiritual growth of the individual seems to depend in some way on the growth of the whole body, while the growth of the whole body requires the spiritual growth of its members (including, for example, their appropriate use of their spiritual gifts). This is easy to miss in the individualism of American Christianity, but the spiritual growth of the body *as a whole* is an important part of this passage.

This immediate passage from Ephesians also does not explicitly mention the Holy Spirit as the one who brings about that growth (though the Spirit is mentioned earlier in Ephesians 4:4). Yet in the context of other passages (for example, 1 Corinthians 12:7–11), we are told that evangelism, teaching, prophecy, etc., which *are* mentioned in verse 11 as part of our growth, are indeed spiritual gifts. Thus, we use the term *spiritual growth* (along with spiritual transformation and spiritual renewal explored in the previous chapter) to describe the entire process of Christian discipleship. 1 Peter 2:2–3, 2 Peter 3:18, Hebrews 6:1, and 1 Corinthians 13:11 also speak of spiritual growth and maturity using the metaphor of person growing and maturing from childhood to adulthood: in the language of Aslan, "getting bigger."

I think Lewis's insight here, conveyed in the words of Aslan, is simple but profound. As Lucy gets bigger, so does her perception of Aslan. As we get bigger, so does our understanding of God. Which is to say, the more we grow spiritually, the bigger God will appear. We do not serve a small God. We serve a God who can do exceedingly beyond all that we ask and think. The more we allow the Holy Spirit to work in our lives—or in Narnian terms, the more one sits in the presence of Aslan and allows his breath on them—the bigger our vision of God. And this leads to another observation about Aslan's breath (and the work of the Holy Spirit) seen both in the previous passage about Aslan's breath as well as the next one.

BECOMING BRAVE IN THE BREATH OF ASLAN

The second reference to Aslan's breath in *Prince Caspian* comes when all four Pevensie children appear face to face with Aslan (Chapter 11). Susan's encounter with Aslan is particularly noteworthy in the context of this book. "Then, after an awful pause, the deep voice said, 'Susan.' Susan made no answer but the others thought she was crying. 'You have listened to fears, child,' said Aslan. 'Come, let me breathe on you. Forget them. Are you brave again?'"

The New Testament tell us that the Holy Spirit gives faith, frees us from the power of fear, and gives us courage. In promising the Holy Spirit, and looking ahead to the day of Pentecost, Jesus told his disciples, "But you will receive power when the Holy Spirit comes on you; and you will be my witnesses in Jerusalem, and in all Judea and Samaria, and to the ends of the earth" (Acts 1:8). It is not long before we begin to see this promise fulfilled. Acts 4 tells of religious leaders (in this case the Sadducees, with the help of the temple guard) arresting Peter and John—seizing them and throwing them in jail. Keeping in mind the crucifixion that Jesus had just suffered, Peter and John had plenty of reason to be afraid, especially when brought before the high priest to be questioned. Yet we read that Peter, "filled with the Holy Spirit," makes a powerful defense of his faith (4:8–12). The response of the religious leaders is telling. "When they saw the courage of Peter and John and realized that they were unschooled, ordinary men, they were astonished and they took note that these men had been with Jesus" (Acts 4:13). The religious leaders note the courage of Peter and John. They attribute that courage to Peter and John having been with Jesus. Luke has already given us the important additional information. It is not merely some natural or intellectual change in Peter and John that came from hearing Jesus' ideas. There has been a spiritual change. They have been filled with the Holy Spirit, who has in turn filled them with courage and boldness.

A little later in Acts 4:31, we read of an even larger group of Jesus' followers: "After they prayed, the place where they were meeting was shaken. And they were all filled with the Holy Spirit and spoke the word of God boldly." Keep in mind that not many days before this, the disciples were terrified and hiding. Now their fear has left them. They have become bold. This, we are told, came about because they were filled with the Holy Spirit. It is the Holy Spirit who takes away their fear and gives courage in its place. The 2 Timothy 1:6–7 passage cited in the previous chapter gets at the same idea, speaking of the Spirit giving us power, love, and self-discipline (rather than timidity).

C.S. Lewis has beautifully illustrated this first in Lucy, then in Susan, and then in Edmund. All three grew in the boldness and courage—and most importantly, the faith—needed to obey Aslan despite the dangers and opposition to doing so, which in Edmund's case included walking into the midst of the enemy camp.

The fourth and final passage in *Prince Caspian* referencing Aslan's breath gets at something similar. This time we see a sort of spiritual growth and newfound courage in a new follower of Aslan. We see that one taking the very first baby steps of faith can still experience the empowering presence of the Spirit, which Lewis again illustrates through the symbolism of Aslan's breath. The scene takes place in Chapter 15, the final chapter of the book, when Aslan gives the opportunity for some of the Telmarines to leave Narnia through a "magic" door and return to their own world. When Aslan asks for volunteers, most of the Telmarines lack either the faith or the courage to step forward. But we read of one unnamed volunteer from among the Telmarine soldiers.

> "Well, I'll take the offer."
> "It is well chosen," said Aslan. "And because you have spoken first, strong magic is upon you. Your future in that world shall be good. Come forth."
> The man, now a little pale, came forward. Aslan and his court drew aside, leaving him free access to the empty doorway of the stakes.
> "Go through it, my son," said Aslan, bending toward him and touching the man's nose with his own. As soon as the Lion's breath came about him, a new look came into man's eyes—startled but not unhappy—as if he were trying to remember something. Then he squared his shoulders and walked into the Door.

Here we have another reference to the "magic" of Aslan, and one that reinforces what I wrote earlier about Lewis's use of the word. In this case, Aslan himself uses the word, and he uses it explicitly as a spiritual blessing, speaking good into the life of this man and his future. The reference to magic is immediately followed by Aslan breathing on the man. Thus, we see that this sort of magic associated with Aslan is a spiritual thing: a blessing, but even more than that; through his breath, Aslan seems to impart his Holy Spirit on this new follower who has demonstrated the first steps of faith (albeit with no little trepidation and doubt). And, as with Lucy, Susan, and Edmund, the result of Aslan's breath on the man is a newfound courage and boldness. A new look in his face. A squaring of his shoulders. And then obedience to the call of Aslan.

III

Blended Symbols and More Courage

"You are too old, children, and you must begin to come close to your own world now." We are at the end of the story of *The Voyage of the Dawn Treader,* at the eastern edge of the world on the borders of Aslan's own country. Here in the final two pages of the book we have our first and only appearance of Aslan in physical form and close proximity to Edmund, Lucy, and Eustace all together at the same time—though Aslan's words are addressed specifically to Edmund and Lucy. Despite the success of the quest, they are sad words. Sad for the two Pevensies, and sad too for many readers. Edmund and Lucy will not return to Narnia.

"It isn't Narnia, you know," sobbed Lucy. "It's you. We shan't meet you there. And how can we live, never meeting you?"

"But you shall meet me, dear one," said Aslan.

"Are—are you there too, Sir?" said Edmund.

"I am," said Aslan. "But there I have another name. You must learn to know me by that name. This was the very reason why you were brought to Narnia, that by knowing me here for a little, you may know me better there."

"And is Eustace never to come back here either?" said Lucy.

"Child," said Aslan, "do you really need to know that? Come, I am opening the door in the sky." Then all in one moment there was a rending of the blue wall (like a curtain being torn) and a terrible white light from beyond the sky, and the feel of Aslan's mane and a Lion's kiss on their foreheads and then—the back bedroom in Aunt Alberta's home at Cambridge.

If readers have not yet guessed that "other name" by which Aslan is known in our world—or even that he can be known in our world—this scene surely brings us closer. Moments earlier, before taking incarnate bodily form as a lion, Aslan had revealed himself as a lamb: another clear connection between him and the Second Person of the Trinity as we know him in our world, as noted in the opening chapter of this book.

With regard to our exploration of the imagery of Aslan's breath, the significant observation here is that Aslan's appearances are few and brief in *The Voyage of the Dawn Treader,* with no *explicit* mention of Aslan's breath—nothing more than this brief reference at the end of the story to "the feel of Aslan's mane and a Lion's kiss on their foreheads."

Now the kiss here (reminiscent of the lick in the first book, and the light touch of the tongue in the second) does seem to be a symbol of anointing. In this case, it is an anointing of Lucy and Edmund for a new task Aslan has just given to them: learning to know him by the name he has in their world (which is our world), even as they begin to come close to their own world—presumably for the sake of ministering in and to that world. The kiss may or may not imply Aslan's breath along with that kiss. (It's hard for me to imagine such a kiss without it accompanied also by a breath.) But even if Aslan's kiss does imply Aslan's breath, the passage says nothing about the *impact* of that breath. (We won't have to get too far into the next book in the series before we see the impact. But that discussion will have to wait.)

So why do my book need this chapter at all if there is no reference to the *ruach elohim*? As it turns out, this book has what is the most complex and multifaceted blended symbolic portrayal of the Holy Spirit of any of the Narnia books—one very worth exploration.

LIFE'S EPISODIC JOURNEYS

Although there are unifying themes binding together the seven volumes of the Chronicles of Narnia, each book also explores different themes in different ways. In terms of the narrative structure, *The Voyage of the Dawn Treader* is the most episodic. If made into a streaming series, each island adventure along along with the sea serpent adventure could be a separate episode, and—with the exception of Eustace's dragoning and un-dragoning, which is a central moment in his character growth that greatly impacts his later behavior—the ordering of the episodes would not be especially important.

In terms of Lewis's portrayal of the Holy Spirit, another unique and important aspect of *The Voyage of the Dawn Treader* is the centrality of a journey. In *The Lion, the Witch and the Wardrobe* and *Prince Caspian*, the children do travel around Narnia on foot but there is no overarching destination that defines a goal. And those travels, while offering challenges and opportunities for growth, take up a smaller part of the story.[5] *The Horse and His Boy* involves a long journey of escape for Shasta and Aravis, but while Shasta ends up saving Archenland from invasion, and he eventually becomes its king, he did not set out from Calormen to do so. The two children are journeying *away* from something as much as they are journeying *toward* something. Near the end of *The Magician's Nephew*, Digory is given a task involving travel, but his journey takes only two chapters to recount, and he wasn't called to Narnia for the sake of that task. Rather, the quest is thrust upon him because of his earlier bad choices. *The Last Battle* involves very little travel for its child protagonists Eustace and Polly; most of the story takes place in or near the stable, and there is no overarching quest other than trying to help Tirian.

The Voyage of the Dawn Treader and *The Silver Chair* are the only two Narnia book in which the child protagonists, from the start of the book, have a defined quest necessitating travel—and in which the journey takes up essentially the entire book. But these two books have a significant difference. In *The Silver*

---

5   In *The Lion, the Witch and the Wardrobe*, the four Pevensies set out across Narnia in Chapter 6 but their goals keep changing, and their travel ends by the start of Chapter 12—taking up only about one third of the book. Similarly, in *Prince Caspian* it isn't even until Chapter 8 that the Pevensies have any idea at all what the real problem is, and even then they have only a vague sense of what they are supposed to do. Their journey across Narnia takes less than four of fifteen chapters.

Chair, the journey is a classic there-and-back-again quest with the task itself being central to every element of the quest, as suggested by the book's title. While Caspian and the crew of the eponymous ship in *The Voyage of the Dawn Treader* are on a sort of quest, it is more of a quest of discovery and exploration than of trying to accomplish some important mission vital to Narnia. As suggest by the book's title, the voyage rather than the task is central thing. And the overarching mission (such as it is) is more the quest of King Caspian and his crew than of the three children; Lucy and Edmund (and a reluctant Eustace) are just along for the ride with no "and-back-again" to follow the "there." The specific task of waking the remaining three Telmarine lords from enchanted sleep doesn't even arise until the thirteenth of sixteen chapters.

So why is this worth mentioning? I am not the first to say that life is a journey. Like the three children in *The Voyage of the Dawn Treader,* we begin our journey getting drawn by hands from dark waters of mystery up (we hope) into some community we call a family, and ending (we hope) in Aslan's Country. Moreover, although many of us as adults may seek to grow in character or faith or maturity, we don't necessarily take the journey with some specific lifelong goal that defines all our choices: a particular task we need to accomplish, and when we have accomplished it we are done. At least for me, the life journey seems far more episodic. We have an elementary school episode, a middle school episode, and a high school episode. Some of us may have a college episode. We may have many different job episodes over the course of our journey. Perhaps a marriage episode or episodes, each of which can be divided into myriad smaller episodes. Each year, each month, each week, even each day can feel like a separate little island adventure episode.

And we ask how the Holy Spirit is present with us and working in us through that episodic journey of life. When we ask the question in that way, then *The Voyage of the Dawn Treader* maybe provides the best narrative structure of any of the seven books for exploring that question.

A CONSPICUOUS ABSENCE

Another interesting aspect of *The Voyage of Dawn Treader*—and one that might seem slightly troublesome in light of the previous paragraph—is how little readers see of Aslan in any physically incarnate form. Consider briefly Aslan's appearances in this book other than the scene at the end of story with which we began this chapter: a scene that takes place on the borders of his own country.

Aslan appears to Eustace to tear off his dragon skin (Chapter 7), but only Eustace sees him; the other characters in the story (and even the readers!) only hear about him through Eustace's third person account. Aslan then appears for just an instant—a single paragraph of the story—on Deathwater Island (Chapter 8), and then disappears. Although he makes up for the brevity of this appearance with tremendous size ("He was the size of an elephant"), the imagery again makes this appearance more like a vision than the physically incarnate Aslan of previous stories: his passing makes no noise; he appears and disappears mysteriously with the narrator stating that "nobody ever saw how or where he went"; his form is "shining as if he were in bright sunlight"; and when he departs those who saw him are described as being "like people waking from sleep," which (as noted in the introduction to this book) hints at something more like a dream or a vision; and finally, a sort of forgetfulness also falls over those who saw him "for the memory of the last hour had all become confused," which leads Drinian to describe them as seeming "a bit bewitched."

Aslan makes a third appearance to Lucy in the house of the magician Coriakin on the island of the Dufflepuds (Chapters 10 and 11), though as noted earlier he is invisible through most of the scene and Lucy (as well as the reader) only becomes aware of him at the end. Lucy does speak with him then, much as she did in the woods at nighttime in *Prince Caspian,* but then "instantly he was vanished away," as though it had been yet another vision. In the final chapter (Chapter 16), Aslan appears to Caspian, but again it is in a vision speaking to Caspian out of a carved image of himself.

The scenes in which Aslan appears (often just to a single character) are also the moments of great *spiritual* need in the story. I think of when Eustace's greed has turned him into a dragon and he cannot save or transform himself; Aslan appears to save Eustace, though Eustace must consent to his saving. I think of the spiritual danger to the entire company caused by Edmund's and Caspian's lust for gold on Goldwater Island—later renamed Deathwater Island—and the near-deadly conflict between them; Aslan again appears, possibly in a vision, and somehow turns them away from their evil. I think of Lucy's moment of temptation in Coriakin's house; Aslan appears to Lucy in a vision in the pages of the magician's book, and reminds her of who she is and who he is, and thus helps her to recognize her temptation and turn from it. And I think of Caspian's moment of selfish, prideful, temptation near the end of the book when he initially refuses to let Reepicheep sail to the end of the world; and, yes, Aslan also appears to Caspian—this time in a vision from his picture frame—and also turns him away from his evil choice. All of these are examples of the spiritual dangers caused primarily by sin and pride. They are also examples of how Aslan's post-resurrection appearances might themselves (apart from his breath) be pointers toward the work of the Holy Spirit—but while this paragraph may hint at where we are going, that discussion will have to wait until the final chapter of this book.

THE BREATH OF ASLAN, WITHOUT THE LION

The one passage in *The Voyage of the Dawn Treader* especially important to our topic takes place on the Dark Island, which to me has always been the most frightening (though not the saddest[6]) moment of all the Narnia stories. In contrast to the scenes mentioned in the previous section, on the Dark Island the grave danger is an external force of darkness rather than the sinful nature of one of the characters in the story. And it is in that scene that we catch the powerful two-fold image of the Holy Spirit.

Before looking at that passage, let us turn first to the scene of Jesus' baptism

---

6   The saddest passages for me in all the Narnia stories—the ones that will make me weep every time I read them—are the descriptions of the animals turning away from Aslan in *The Last Battle* because they have been deceived or betrayed by the false Aslan and either no longer believe in Aslan at all or believe that he is evil.

described in the Gospel of Mark which helped me make the most sense of Lewis's complex imagery of the Holy Spirit. We need consider just two verses from this passage: "Just as Jesus was coming up out of the water, he saw heaven being torn open and the Spirit descending on him like a dove. And a voice came from heaven: 'You are my Son, whom I love; with you I am well pleased'" (Mark 1:10-11[7]). Though there is much we could discuss regarding John's baptism of his cousin Jesus, three observations hold particular importance for this chapter. First, we see Heaven torn open. What would it look like to see Heaven torn open? How would anybody at Jesus' baptism have known to describe it as such? I have always imagined a sort of rending or opening of the skies, and a momentary but powerful shining through of God's glory like a blinding ray of light. Second, the Holy Spirit descends on Jesus in the form of a dove—a white bird. Many famous paintings of the scene (such as Baptism of Christ painted by Andrea del Verrocchio and Leonardo da Vinci) picture the dove in the air over Jesus. However, I have always imagined the dove alighting on Jesus' shoulder. Third, we hear a voice, seeming to come out of Heaven.

Do you remember the start of the scene when Lucy and the others on the Dawn Treader are rescued from the Dark Island (Chapter 12)? The sky opens up. A bird descends. A voice speaks. Consider this in more detail. The rescuing begins with a spot of light in the sky—or in the heavens, we might say. The English word "heaven" comes to us from an Old English word *heofen,* which originally meant the visible expanse of sky and later came to mean the home of God. The Greek word *OURANOUS* used in Mark 1:10 has a similar history. It means the expanse of the sky and all that is visible within it, but it was used symbolically to represent the place where God rules. The narration in Chapter 12 describes the deliverance of the Dawn Treader from the Dark Island from Lucy's perspective. It begins, "There was a tiny speck of light ahead, and while they watched a broad beam of light fell from it upon the ship. It did not alter the surrounding darkness, but the whole ship was lit up as if by a searchlight." Doesn't that read like Heaven being torn open, and its glory shining down upon the ship?

---

7   The accounts in Matthew 3:16–17 and Luke 3:21–22 are nearly identical except Luke's account also mentions that Jesus was praying.

Then Lucy sees something in the beam of light. "At first it looked like a cross, then it looked like an aeroplane, then it looked like a kite, and at last with a whirring of wings it was right overhead and was an albatross. It circled three times round the mast and then perched for an instant on the crest of the gilded dragon at the prow." The image of a cross must remind the Christian reader of Christ. As the object gets closer, it comes into clearer focus. It is a bird. This bird that comes and leads them to safety is not a dove (which would have been a more obvious symbol of the Holy Spirit). Yet it is a white bird, and it clearly descends from Heaven and alights—not on any one person, but on the ship itself.

And then comes the voice. It is a strong sweet voice, though in the case of Lewis's story readers are not initially told what words are spoken or even if there are words or language, but only that the voice conveyed "what seemed to be words though no one understood them." Ah! But later we are told what some of the words were, for Lucy did hear them. It was speech after all. "Courage, dear heart," the voice says.

Is this another example of Lewis portraying (or pointing readers toward) the Third Person of the Trinity, though in a different way from the kiss and breath of Aslan? There are enough parallels here between this scene of the albatross in *The Voyage of the Dawn Treader* and that of the Holy Spirit who comes in the form of a dove at the baptism of Jesus to suggest this. But in case we missed it, Lewis gives us another hint, blending together two pointers to or symbols or images of the Spirit in one scene. For we read that somehow, mysteriously, Lucy feels the breath of Aslan on her. "Lucy knew that as it circled the mast it had whispered to her, 'Courage, dear heart,' and the voice, she felt sure, was Aslan's, and with the voice a delicious smell breathed in her face." A breath may carry a smell, but smells themselves do not breathe. If it was the voice of Aslan (as Lucy felt sure it was), then it was also Aslan's breath "with the voice." Here, again, is the image of Aslan's breath, though Lewis comes at the image in a less direct way.

WHAT THE SPIRIT GIVES

So far, we have looked only at the imagery itself—Aslan's breath and the white bird that descends from the heavens—and how it seems to point to the Holy Spirit. But what does Lewis do with this imagery? What does he illustrate

·

about the work or character of the Holy Spirit? One way to answer that question is to ask: *What does the Holy Spirit give to Lucy—and to the others on the ship?*

I think there are multiple answers to this question; it is not just one thing. Perhaps most importantly, the Spirit gives them a reminder that God is there, present with them. He provides a reminder that they are not alone. Though they walk—or, rather, sail—through the shadow of death, they need not fear for God is with them. And he loves them. He will never forsake them. He will never forsake *us*. Courage, dear heart. The Holy Spirit is, indeed, the presence of God with us at all times, including the darkest times. Through all the scenes and moments of our long episodic journey of life.

That presence—which is to say, the spirit of Aslan in the form of the albatross—eventually leads them all back from darkness to the light. That is the second thing the Spirit gives: guidance. First courage. Then guidance. Lucy, and Caspian, and the sailors aboard the Dawn Treader need only to follow the albatross. "Drinian steered after it not doubting that it offered good guidance.. .. In a few moments the darkness turned into greyness ahead, and then, almost before they dared to begin hoping, they had shot out into the sunlight and were in the warm, blue world again. And all at once everybody realised that there was nothing to be afraid of and never had been."

It is interesting to me that the albatross that seems to be the very presence of Aslan makes no specific promise to Lucy. The voice does not say how long the darkness will last. It does not even promise safety. It does two things: it calls Lucy to courage, and it calls her to follow. The darkness does not immediately go away. Nor are we told that Lucy's fear immediately vanishes, only that they have the courage to continue despite their fear. What a powerful and much needed reminder! Only when they come out into the light do they realize they needn't have been afraid in the first place. But the albatross—Aslan, the Holy Spirit—does not chastise or cast shame on them for having been afraid. He only calls them to courage.

A couple of years ago, while I was working on my book *Disciple Making in a Culture of Power, Comfort, and Fear,* I concluded that "do not fear" is the most oft-repeated command in Scripture—especially if you count all the many variations such as "be courageous" and "do not be afraid" and "fear not." Not that this makes it the most important command: Jesus affirmed that loving the Lord God and loving our neighbors were the two most important commands (Matthew 22:37–40) that provide a foundation for all other commands. Still, we must see that turning away from fear is an important way to obey God. When we incite fear in others—which, sadly, is a popular political and religious ploy used to manipulate voters and followers—we turn them away from how God would have them live. We do evil when we promote fear. It is the Holy Spirit who gives freedom from fear, who gives us the power to obey the command "do not fear," and who repeatedly says to us, "Courage, dear heart."

The Lord is indeed our Shepherd. He gives us everything we need. Though we walk through the valley of the shadow of death—or sail through the dark island of the shadow of death—we need not fear. God is with us. The Holy Spirit is with us. As those aboard the Dawn Treader realize, "there was nothing to be afraid of and never had been."

We could end this chapter here, or maybe the entire book. There might not be any application in Lewis's portrayal of the Holy Spirit in Narnia more important than that one given to Lucy by the voice of Aslan speaking through the albatross: Courage, *dear heart.* And in any case, as already noted, there is no other mention of Aslan's breath in *The Voyage of the Dawn Treader.* Yet it is worth returning once more to the scene at end of the book in which Aslan anoints the three children with a kiss and sends them back to their world. In that closing scene Lewis seems to be pointing at one more important aspect of the work of the Holy Spirit, though without a mention of Aslan's breath. As already noted, the scene begins with Edmund, Lucy, and Eustace finding Aslan on the shore cooking a meal of fish—much how Jesus' disciple Peter came upon Jesus after the resurrection. Initially, Aslan appears in the form of a lamb. Lucy speaks first. "Please, Lamb, is this the way to Aslan's country?" The lamb replies, "Not for you. For you the door into Aslan's country is from your own world." This sets the stage for the final scene, for it raises the question for Lucy and Edmund of how they will find the door. And then, equally importantly, how they will know Aslan himself.

"Oh, Aslan," said Lucy. "Will you tell us how to get into your country from our world?"

"I shall be telling you all the time," said Aslan. "But I will not tell you how long or short the way will be; only that it lies across a river. But do not fear that, for I am the great Bridge Builder. And now come; I will open the door in the sky and send you to your own land." . . .

"You must learn to know me by that name. This was the very reason why you were brought to Narnia."

It is after this that Aslan anoints them with a kiss. (Only Edmund and Lucy are mentioned, but Eustace is present also. The "them" thus seems to refer to all three children.) If this anointing goes hand in hand with the imparting of the Spirit—that is to say, with the breath of Aslan—then Lewis is also pointing out something very important about the work of the Holy Spirit: that work is to reveal God to us all.

We can know Aslan by the name he goes by in our world. And in knowing God, we can also know the way to God's kingdom—the way to Aslan's country. For that way is Jesus himself. He is not only the way, but also the truth and the life.

IV

THE SILVER CHAIR

Carried on Aslan's Breath

As noted in the previous chapter, of the seven Narnia books *The Silver Chair* most closely fits the mold of a quest narrative: a there-and-back-again-with-a-given-purpose journey. Aslan has given to Eustace and Jill the specific task of rescuing Prince Rilian from the enchantment of the Emerald Witch and returning him to his father, King Caspian, before Caspian dies. That task takes up the entire narrative. It involves a journey on foot that is far longer than the journeys taken by the Pevensies in either *The Lion, the Witch and the Wardrobe* or *Prince Caspian*. That literal walk also works as a wonderful metaphor for aspects of the spiritual journey that followers of Christ are on—a journey which Jesus, Paul, and John all referred to metaphorically as a "walk" (John 11:9–10, 12:35; Galatians 5:16; Ephesians 5:2; 1 John 1:6–7).

At the start of the story, even before the first mention of Aslan's breath, readers catch a glimpse of Aslan's impact on the lives of those who follow him. We see this in the change that has been wrought in Eustace since his interactions with Aslan in *The Voyage of the Dawn Treader*. Those changes began with a personal and intimate interaction when Aslan freed Eustace from his dragon skin, and they continued over the remainder of that voyage. In the final scene at the end of that previous book, Eustace is sent back to his own world with an anointing kiss from Aslan and the goal of knowing him better. The final paragraph tells readers that "back in his own world everyone soon started saying how Eustace had improved, and how 'You'd never know him for the same boy.'"

The Silver Chair begins by recognizing that transformation. The changes in Eustace are visible to Jill who in the first chapter agrees that Eustace is "different chap" than he used to be, less of a "little tick." Seeking more affirmation of this difference—what readers might describe as a spiritual transformation— Eustace asks, "You think there has been a change, then?" Jill's reply reaffirms it. "It's not only me. Everyone's been saying so." Aslan has breathed on Eustace. The spirit of the Lion is present in the boy. Even as the Holy Spirit transforms and renews those who follow Christ, so also is Eustace being transformed. Though, as the rest of the book reveals, there is still some transformational work to be done in him, even as there is in all of us readers.

And this leads us to the portrayal of Aslan's breath in *The Silver Chair*. Does this fourth book in the Chronicles of Narnia contain any additional pointers to the Holy Spirit? Again, the answer is yes—though I almost didn't write this chapter. That I did is partly thanks to members of the New York C.S. Lewis Society (especially Erin Seidel) for suggesting that I do. In my presentation to that group in March of 2023 (mentioned in my introduction), I only quickly skimmed over *The Silver Chair*. This was partly for reasons of limited presentation time, and partly because I initially focused only on the transporting power of Aslan's breath which carries first Eustace and then Jill across the sea from Aslan's country in the high mountains beyond the eastern edge of the world to the shores of Narnia. While there is *something* interesting in that unique display of power, it turns out there is much more than that—more that I might not have taken the time to explore had I not been encouraged to delve deeper.

SUPERNATURAL POWER EXHIBITED IN THE NATURAL WORLD

We don't have to read far into *The Silver Chair* to find references to Aslan's breath. Chapter 1 begins behind the gym at the Experimental School (where both Eustace and Jill are students) and ends at the cliff where Eustace falls. Immediately after he falls, Aslan appears beside Jill and begins to blow. His breath, we later learn, will carry Eustace across the ocean from Aslan's country all the way to Narnia. Jill doesn't know this, however. She only sees Eustace fall (a first reason for terror), and then looks over and sees a giant lion right beside her (a second reason for terror). The narrator describes this scene from Jill's perspective. "[The lion] was lying down, leaning over; and (this was the odd thing) blowing. Not roaring or snorting, but just blowing from its wide-opened mouth; blowing out as steadily as a vacuum cleaner sucks in. Jill was lying so close to the creature that she could feel the breath vibrating steadily through its body." The passage uses the verb "blowing" three times. Of course, blowing is a type of breathing—a purposeful and forceful breathing—and Lewis could have left it at that, allowing readers to make their own connection to breath. But then the narrator explicitly references Aslan's breath. The image of breath which is *invisible*, "vibrating steadily through [Aslan's] body," connects that breath with the fullness of Aslan as a *visible* bodily creature in the same incarnate form of a lion that he assumes when in Narnia.

The scene repeats in Chapter 2—though thankfully without the terror of somebody falling off the cliff. The second time, it is Jill who travels across the sea. "Please," she asks the lion, "how am I to get to Narnia?" Aslan replies, "On my breath." The narrator makes no mention of blowing now; the language is fully back to Aslan's breath.

When I pondered this scene in light of Aslan's breath, considering it as a possible pointer to the Holy Spirit, my initial thought was of the account of Philip and the Ethiopian official (Acts 8:26–40). That biblical scene begins with an angel telling Philip to go out to a certain desert road. Philip obeys, and there he meets the Ethiopian official passing by on his way home after a trip to Jerusalem. Luke's account does not tell us much about the Ethiopian man except that he was both an important treasury official and also a eunuch, and that he had gone to Jerusalem to worship God. When Philip encountered him, he was sitting in his chariot reading Scripture aloud. So we surmise that the Ethiopian was in some way or another a seeker of God; he was trying to learn about God, and to understand God's word. Hearing the man read from the prophet Isaiah, Philip began to explain both Isaiah and the gospel to him. He connected Isaiah 53:7–8 to the good news of Jesus Christ. After some conversation, the Ethiopian decided to be baptized. And that's where the story gets wondrously strange. As soon as they were out of the water, "the Spirit of the Lord suddenly took Philip away and the eunuch did not see him again, but went on his way rejoicing" (Acts 8:39).

I wonder about many things here, including how Luke knew that the eunuch went on his way "rejoicing" if the eunuch never saw Philip again. But my biggest questions are about what happened to Philip—what it felt like for him, and what his departure (or disappearance) looked like to the Ethiopian. Philip didn't merely become invisible and then slowly walk away; Luke tells us that the Spirit "suddenly took Philip away." Did Philip teleport to a new location? Did he become like a particle of light and move at lightspeed? Was he lifted up and carried off by the wind? Any of those would have been miraculous, though possible for the God who created the universe, light, and even time itself. Yet we don't know what the *mechanism* of travel was. We only know that Philip disappeared from the desert and then "appeared at Azotus and traveled about, preaching the gospel," and that it was the Spirit of the Lord who brought him to Azotus (Acts 8:40). Although the words "suddenly" and the casual but mysterious use of the word "appeared" have always made me imagine a sort of instantaneous teleporting, the mode of travel doesn't really matter. However fast or even instantaneous his travel was, what to me seems clear and important is that the Spirit of the Lord *supernaturally moved Philip* from one place to another. Depending on where along the road from Jerusalem to Gaza that Philip met the Ethiopian, the miraculous trip was likely between twenty-five and forty miles. The power of the Holy Spirit doesn't work only in some spiritual realm, but in the physical world of flesh and matter.

Perhaps in the breath of Aslan carrying the two children across the ocean, Lewis was attempting to capture the same truths that the story of Philip conveys about the Holy Spirit. Keep in mind that these two stories—Eustace and Jill traveling on Aslan's breath and the Spirit transporting Philip to Azotus—are nearly singular events in both Narnian history and biblical history.[8] The closest

---

8   I am not counting angelic appearances since angels are not described as having the same sorts of physical bodies made of the dust of the earth. Nor do I count the supernatural post-resurrection appearances of Jesus who seemed to move about without consideration of space or walls. We can also discount the bodily departures of Enoch and Elijah at the end of their earthly lives, as they seem to have vanished directly to Heaven rather than being transported somewhere else on earth.

similar example in the Bible is a story involving Jesus after his miraculous feeding of the five thousand somewhere on the eastern shore of the Sea of Galilee (John 6:1–15). His disciples, having departed by boat leaving Jesus praying alone on a mountain, have gone "about three or four miles" when Jesus comes walking out across the water to join them (6:19). John's account does not tell us exactly where on the eastern shore the miraculous feeding took place, but since the Sea of Galilee is a little over six miles wide (east to west) and about thirteen miles long (north to south), their journey back to Capernaum (on the northwest coast) would have been between six and thirteen miles long. The disciples have gone less than half that distance when Jesus appears, walking across the water. Walking on water is itself already a miraculous mode of travel, but once Jesus gets into the boat we read of something even stranger that involves not just Jesus but all of the disciples and even the boat: "immediately the boat reached the shore where they were heading" (John 6:21). As with Luke's use of the word "suddenly" in the story of Philip, the word "immediately" seems important here. One moment, the disciples in their boat are between three and ten miles away from their destination. Then *immediately* they are at their destination. John does not tell us how it happened, what the disciples thought about it, or even what he himself thought about it. (What on earth could John have written beyond what he wrote? No words could explain it.) Yet there is no doubt that it was a miraculous mode of transport that did not adhere to normal observed patterns of our physical universe.

The other analogous scenes of miraculous biblical travel involving humans occur during a brief period in the life of the prophet Elijah (described in 1 Kings 18–19). In this story, the land of Israel has been suffering from a prolonged drought.

Elijah (who had prophesied the drought) was in continued conflict with King Ahab, who is trying to kill him. Elijah has asked a palace administrator named Obadiah to deliver a message to Ahab. Our first hint of supernatural travel comes from the reply of a fearful Obadiah: "But now you tell me to go to my master and say, 'Elijah is here.' I don't know where the Spirit of the LORD may carry you when I leave you. If I go and tell Ahab and he doesn't find you, he will kill me" (1 Kings 18:11–12). We don't know what previous events (if any) triggered that concern in Obadiah. He may only have been speaking out of an unreasoned fear. Yet his words suggest that Elijah had a history of supernatural travel attributed to the Spirit of the Lord.

In any case, two events soon after that give credence to Obadiah's concerns. The first follows the famous confrontation between Elijah and the prophets of Baal and Asherah on Mount Carmel (1 Kings 18:16–46)—the planning for which had prompted the conversation between Elijah and Obadiah in the first place. When the confrontation is over, and the prophets of Baal and Asherah have been put to death, and rain starts falling to end the drought, Ahab starts back to Jezreel *on his chariot*. Then "the power of the LORD came on Elijah and, tucking his cloak into his belt, he ran ahead of Ahab all the way to Jezreel" (18:46). Given that Elijah outruns the king who is riding on a chariot, we can imagine some combination of supernatural speed and supernatural endurance. We know Elijah's journey wasn't done by human strength, because the narrative attributes the travel to "the power of the LORD" coming on him.

We then read of Elijah, just a few days later, traveling for forty days and nights from his broom tree to the mountain in Horeb (1 Kings 19:4–8). There is no indication that Elijah moves supernaturally *fast* in this case (that is, faster than a human could run), but given that he travels day and night (i.e., without rest) for forty days, we are left with little doubt that (at the minimum) he travels with supernatural strength or endurance, and that the entire trip was made miraculously much faster than humanly possible. Going back to the start of 1 Kings 18 and the words of Obadiah, all this supernatural travel is attributed to "the Spirit of the LORD" (1 Kings 18:12) and later also to "the power of the LORD" (1 Kings 18:46) and to the ministering of an "angel of the LORD" (1 Kings 19:7). Again, in both the first and third of those biblical examples (Philip's teleportation and Elijah's pair of journeys on foot), the Holy Spirit or the Spirit of the Lord is referenced as the source of power. In the second one (crossing the Sea of Galilee), Jesus was present. All are examples of supernatural travel beyond any physical explanation, all clearly accomplished by the power of God.

And that was as far as I explored in *The Silver Chair* in my presentation to the New York C.S. Lewis Society. Lewis illustrated that there is power in the breath of Aslan that transcends the normal patterns observed in the material world, even to the point of empowering supernatural travel not unlike what we read about in these few but memorable biblical examples. God is at work in supernatural, miraculous ways in his created world through his Holy Spirit. That is an important reminder and an exciting one. That God has (and has demonstrated) that sort of power should help his people know they need not fear their foes.

There is so much more in this passage, however. Had I had more time (and looked more deeply) I good have given the entire talk about Aslan's breath based only on *The Silver Chair*—and much of it just from the rest of that passage in which Jill floats across the sea on Aslan's breath.

STILLNESS AND LISTENING

We begin this further exploration with a short but important section. The description of the scene in which Aslan's breath carries Jill across the ocean starts with Aslan's instructions to her. "Stand still. In a moment I will blow. But first, remember, remember the signs."

Much of the discussion so far in this book has been about the transforming work of the Holy Spirit in our lives illustrated by the impact of Aslan's breath on various characters: giving them peace, taking away their fear and replacing it with boldness, and helping them follow him and make good choices. Yet earlier we noted Paul's use of the passive voice when he instructed Christians to *be transformed* and renewed. The use of the passive voice as part of a command tells us both that transformation is the work of the Holy Spirit (and not something we can do ourselves), and simultaneously that it calls for our participation and obedience. So how do we participate? More specifically, how do we listen for the Holy Spirit?

Before we even get to Aslan's breath lifting and carrying Jill, his instructions to her offer two important lessons on how she is to participate in his work. The first is the simplest but perhaps the most important (and the hardest to do in a busy life amid a busy world): "Stand still." Listening for the Spirit's voice often requires our stillness. Or, we might say, *hearing* the Spirit requires *listening*. And listening is done best in quiet and stillness. Experiencing the *breath* of Aslan comes when we spend time standing in the *presence* of Aslan. And stillness is our first step: building stillness and listening into our lives: our daily routines, our weekly routines, our annual routines. The shepherd-king-psalmist David tells us (in Psalm 23) that God leads us to green pastures and quiet waters. Yet we so often choose not to follow Him into those still places. Jesus promises rest to the weary (Matthew 11:28), but rather than accepting that gift of rest we so often cling to busy-ness, which increases our weariness.

There are numerous passages in Scripture that encourage rest, stillness, and listening, including the concept of a Sabbath day of rest which God built into the fabric of creation and (by both example and through the Ten Command-ments) called his people to practice. Although in both Jesus' time and in the modern Christian church, Sabbath rest has often been applied legalistically and even oppressively—as a burden rather than a gift—it is still an important practice for those who seek to follow God. In *Christ Plays in Ten Thousand Places,* Eugene Peterson acknowledges legalistic abuse of the Sabbath but goes on to comment on the importance of keeping the Sabbath for those who want to "live appropriately in the creation." His words extend beyond Sabbath rest to the broader importance of stillness. "We must stop running around long enough to see what [God] has done and is doing. We must shut up long enough to hear what he has said and is saying. All our ancestors agree that without silence and stillness there is no spirituality, no God-attentive, God-responsive life" (117–118). Spirituality here does not refer to some vague sort of emotional life but to a life being transformed by the Spirit of God. We need stillness. We need stillness just to begin to know God. Speaking through one of the psalms of the Sons of Korah, God tell us, "Be still and know that I am God" (Psalm 46:10). The ordering of this twofold command suggests that our stillness comes *before* the revelation of

God; first we are still, and then we know that God is God. Stand still. Follow the shepherd to those times beside still waters and in green pastures.

Aslan's next instruction to Jill is "remember the signs." Since some of my early readings of the Chronicles of Narnia many decades ago, and then my later reading to my three sons, it has seemed to me that these instructions were meant to illustrate for readers the importance of meditating on Scripture. The signs that Jill is to remember were the words (or the Word) of Aslan. She is to spend time daily pondering these signs, so that she is ready to apply them on her long journey with Eustace. Thus, the second lesson (or principle) suggested through Aslan's words to Jill is that we need to spend regular time in God's word, knowing, meditating on, and seeking to understand it. Psalm 1:1–3, Psalm 119, and the epistle known as 2 Timothy (especially verses 1:13–14, 2:15, and 3:16–17) are among my favorite (of many) biblical passages encouraging this. In 2 Timothy 2:7, Paul also instructs Timothy to reflect on Paul's own words, and promises that the Lord will give Timothy insights. How? Through the Holy Spirit.

One of the perceptive readers of a draft of this book suggested that this idea can be summarized simply but importantly as "listen and obey." These are important instructions for Christ followers! It also relates to Jesus' final words to his disciples in Matthew 28:18-20—a passage often referred to as the Great Commission. In exhorting his disciples to make more disciples, Jesus tells those immediate disciples to teach the future disciples to obey everything Jesus has commanded. We hear the teaching and we put it into action. We, like Jill, are to listen and obey. That command also comes with the wonderful promise that Jesus is with his disciples "always, to the very end of the age." He is with us through his Holy Spirit.

Here is another way to consider this. Aslan will guide Jill (as the Spirit guides Christ's followers), but that guidance is not always easy to see. There might be signs that Jill will not understand *until* they appear, and that she won't even recognize unless she is actively looking for them—even as there may be aspects of God's Word and promptings of the Holy Spirit that we will not understand at first, and that we may only understand later by the power of the Spirit. As Lewis also illustrates through Jill, it helps to be paying attention and looking for that guidance, so that when we are walking through whatever signs are given to us (like "UNDER ME") we notice and are ready to follow.

Be still and attentive, listening for the promptings of the Spirit. Be willing to wait. Be still and attentive to the Word of God, and let the Spirit give you insights into what it means and how it applies—which might not come until just the moment when that word is ready to bear fruit.

"WALKING" IN THE EMBRACE OF THE HOLY SPIRIT

With these instructions for how Jill is to be ready for his breath, and how she is to participate in his work, Aslan then breathes on her.

> The voice had been growing softer toward the end of this speech and now it faded away altogether. Jill looked behind her. To her astonishment she saw the cliff already more than a hundred yards behind her, and the Lion himself a speck of bright gold on the edge of it. She had been setting her teeth and clenching her fists for a terrible blast of lion's breath; but the breath had really been so gentle that she had not even noticed the moment at which she left the earth.

Here we read two more references to Aslan's breath, and then (for the first time in the series) a lengthy description of what that breath feels like and what it is like to be surrounded by it. A significant and unique aspect of this scene is that Jill doesn't merely experience the *effect* of Aslan's breath (as though it symbolized the *imparting* of his Spirit) but she is actually *in* Aslan's breath for a prolonged period (as though the breath itself was the Spirit).

One thing that jumps out at me in the description is that Aslan's breath is gentle, despite Jill's expectation that it would be feel harsh: like a "terrible blast." How often do we expect God's treatment of us to be harsh? It's as though we pictured God as some sort of cosmic Darth Vader ready to use the Force to compel our obedience through suffering or the threat of suffering. We will return to gentleness in greater depth in the next chapter; for now, we accept Lewis's reminder of how often Jesus is described as gentle.

The description continues in the next paragraph. Before exploring it, we should first ponder one of Jill's first observations: "There was nothing but air for

thousands upon thousands of feet below her." We might pass by this sentence
too easily, especially if we have read the story many times. But imagine the
terror you would feel in such a situation. Jesus' disciple Peter grew very afraid
just walking on water. In this scene, Jill is floating on nothing but air! From a
purely natural point of view, fear would be—well, very natural. Understandable.
Expected. Yet we read, "She felt frightened only for a second. For one thing, the
world beneath her was so very far away that it seemed to have nothing to do
with her." Once again, as with several earlier passages involving Lucy, Susan,
and others, we see that Aslan's breath has the effect of freeing Jill from fear.
This echoes the biblical idea that the Spirit of God (if we let him) helps those
who serve God to follow the oft-repeated biblical mandate: do not fear; do not
be afraid; be courageous.

This passage takes a further step in that it gives a reason that Jill's fright
disappears, which in turn hints at one way the Spirit frees us from fear. For a
moment, Jill sees the world from the height of Aslan's country, which is to say
from a heavenly perspective; the details that might easily have overwhelmed
her or made her fearful are momentarily seen from afar and become much less
overwhelming.

Before going on, it is important to remember that we are incarnate beings
created and called to live in time and space. Details of life are important. We are
called to love our neighbors, our colleagues, our family, our church family. We
do so in the details of everyday life: washing dishes, planting gardens, building
houses, cooking meals, and going to work. Jesus himself came and lived out
the details of a physical existence in the material world he created. He partici-
pated in meals (many of them!) and weddings, and he showed them to be holy
occasions. He healed bodily diseases, fed hungry people, walked on dusty roads,
and drank well water to refresh himself. The details of our lives are the stuff of
God's creation. So often, however, we see *only* the terrifying things right in front
of us. We don't focus on the goodness of daily life, but on the things that make
us afraid or anxious. Ironically, if Jill had been much closer to the ground—say
only a thousand feet up a cliff, or even a hundred feet up—her focus would
have been on the fearful height. Then (Lewis tells us) her fear would have been
much greater. But in this scene, she is looking down from Aslan's country. She is

granted the gift of a heavenly perspective. Her fear disappears.

The passage reminds me of the scene in 2 Kings 6:15–17 when the armies of Aram surround the prophet Elisha. Focusing on the fearful details of a hostile enemy army, without a more heavenly perspective, Elisha's servant grows afraid.

> When the servant of the man of God got up and went out early the next morning, an army with horses and chariots had surrounded the city. "Oh no, my lord! What shall we do?" the servant asked.
>
> "Don't be afraid," the prophet answered. "Those who are with us are more than those who are with them."
>
> And Elisha prayed, "Open his eyes, Lord, so that he may see." Then the Lord opened the servant's eyes, and he looked and saw the hills full of horses and chariots of fire all around Elisha.

For a brief moment, Elisha's servant is able to see the scene with heavenly rather than worldly perspective. Rather than focusing on the causes of fear, he sees what God is doing. Then he knows he need not fear. Aslan's breath will later bring Jill back closer and closer to earth. She will hear "the noise of wave and the crying of seagulls" and smell "the smell of the sea." Those details also matter. The stuff of the earth matters. Jill needs to live those details out on her quest. Eventually Aslan's breath will settle her on the ground where she is dingy and wet. But she doesn't need to focus on the scary details: neither her height above ground nor her fear of falling. Empowered by Aslan's breath to have the perspective of Aslan's Country, Jill sees with new eyes. Her fear goes away.

Unfortunate as it may seem, however, we are rarely granted such physical vision as Jill and Elijah's servant were granted. We never read of anybody else in Narnia other than Jill and Eustace traveling on Aslan's breath and looking down upon the world from the height of Aslan's Country. Likewise, the Bible does not have many accounts (though there are a few) of humans suddenly looking into the supernatural or spiritual realm and seeing God's heavenly armies. Except we *do* see that way through the eyes of faith, and by the power of the Holy Spirit. We are empowered by the Holy Spirit to see with spiritual eyes, and not to be weighed down by the frightening details of the world, which may be one of the perspectives that helps *us* feel less frightened even when the world gives us reasons to fear—helps us to experience *not* the sort of peace that comes from rational analysis of a situation, but instead a peace that transcends our understanding (as we read about in Philippians 4:7). When we see with spiritual eyes and are released from the anxiety that comes from focusing on fearful things, we are free to care *more* (not less) for the details of creation likes meals, and trees, and conversations, and the way God's signs are revealed to us in the stuff of everyday life.

ASLAN IN A VISION

With respect to Aslan's breath as a symbol of, or pointer to, the Holy Spirit, we conclude our exploration of Jill's unique travel experience and the long passage describing it with four final observations. The first is quick but important: Aslan's breath in this scene is certainly more than just warm moist air. No merely physical or natural air would uphold a human body; this breath is something supernatural. It is somehow a vehicle for the very power of Aslan himself.

The second observation is that Jill had already been traveling in the power of Aslan's breath before she even noticed it. Only when she "looked behind her" did she see (with "astonishment") how far she had come. I find valuable wisdom in this imagery. So often, it is only later when I look backward that I see how—and how *far*—the Spirit has already taken me on my journeys.

The third observation becomes clearer as we continue the description of Jill's voyage, and find two more explicit mentions of Aslan's breath.

> For another, floating on the breath of the Lion was so extremely comfortable. She found she could lie on her back or on her face and twist any way she pleased, just as you can in water (if you've learned to float really well). And because she was moving at the same pace as the breath, there was no wind, and the air seemed beautifully warm. It was not in the least like being in an aeroplane, because there was no noise and no vibration.

Remember that in both Old Testament Hebrew and New Testament Greek, the words translated as *breath* or *spirit* can also mean *wind*. The narrative tells us that Jill could feel "no wind," but readers will know there must have been a tremendous wind based on the speed at which she travels—a "great speed" we are later told, enabling her to cover in half a day what it took weeks or months to cross in the *Dawn Treader*. Yet Jill doesn't feel the wind. What she feels is comfortable. She is so comfortable, in fact, that she falls asleep for several hours, laying "back on the air as if it was a sofa, with a sigh of contentment." Up to this point, Jill has experienced plenty of terror and trauma beginning with the bullying behind the gym, followed by Eustace's fall, then the terrible thirst, and a giant lion whom she fears might eat her. (Keep in mind that prior to that scene, Jill knew nothing about Aslan.) Her task must also have seemed daunting, and of course she had the fear of the journey itself. They story begins with Jill in distress and crying, and until she is lifted on Aslan's breath, she has not had even a moment of relief. Yet Aslan's breath surrounds her so completely that she doesn't even feel the wind. She feels no noise. No vibration. Instead, she experiences contentment and comfort—two of the ways this passage describes her experience. It is a lovely description of being in the embrace of the Holy Spirit. On Aslan's breath, Jill has found what she probably needed most at this difficult time in her life's experience: stillness, peace, and comfort.

"Comfort" in terms of material possessions—that is, being overly comfortable in a worldly sense—can become an idol or temptation leading us away from Christ. Indeed, later in *The Silver Chair,* the promise of "steaming baths, soft beds, and bright hearths" as well as meals of "the roast and the baked and the sweet and the strong" (Chapter 6) do become a temptation that temporarily turns Jill, Eustace, and Puddleglum from their task.

Yet there is another meaning of "comfort": the type of comfort that God's Spirit gives to us; the comfort we need when we feel sorrow; the comfort of having somebody listen to us when we are in distress, and walk alongside of us when we feel trouble or heartache. In his Sermon on the Mount, Jesus said "Blessed are those who mourn, for they will be comforted" (Matthew 5:4). In John 14:16, John uses the Greek word *paraclete* to record Jesus' promise of the coming Holy Spirit. Although the NIV translates *paraclete* as "Advocate" and the NAS translates the word as "Helper," several English translations opt for "Comforter." Jesus who has promised the blessing of comfort for those who mourn has also promised the coming of the Holy Spirit as our great Comforter. For Jill, Aslan's breath brought her comfort after her own time of hardship, fear, and loss.

Yet even as Jill experiences peace and comfort in the embrace of Aslan's breath, she also senses a prompting to meditate on Aslan's words. And that is our fourth and final observation. "By Jove! The signs!" Jill says, after she has been floating for a while on Aslan's breath. "I'd better repeat them." The narrator tells us that "she was in a panic for a second or two, but she found she could still say them all correctly." One way to know whether we are listening to the Holy Spirit speaking to us (as opposed to some other voice) is whether the voice points us back toward God and God's word. (We will also return to this important topic in the final chapter.) The prompting Jill hears while fully experiencing the breath of Aslan points her back to Aslan and Aslan's words. And this leads us to the next—and penultimate—reference to Aslan's breath in *The Silver Chair*.

Almost the entire story is told through Jill's perspective. The most notable exception is when Rilian, Puddleglum, Eustace, and Jill are escaping the underground, and Jill disappears up a hole (in a chapter appropriately titled "The Disappearance of Jill"), leaving the reader with the other three characters for a few short paragraphs. Other than that, we experience the adventure through Jill's eyes. We travel across the sea on Aslan's breath with Jill, but not with Eustace. It is also Jill who next experiences Aslan's breath in the House of Harfang (Chapter 8), one of the most dangerous moments of the story. In this scene, Jill is seemingly in a dream and awakes to see "a lion, The Real Lion, just as she had seen him on the mountain beyond the world's end. And a smell of all sweet-smelling things there are filled the room." The dream starts out nicely, but soon turns troublesome.

> But there was some trouble in Jill's mind, though she could not think what it was, and the tears streamed down her face and wet the pillow. The Lion told her to repeat the signs, and she found that she had forgotten them all. At that, a great horror came over her. And Aslan took her up in his jaws (she could feel his lips and his breath but not his teeth) and carried her to the window and made her look out. The moon shone bright; and written in great letters across the world or the sky (she did not know which) were the words UNDER ME. After that, the dream faded away, and when she woke, very late next morning, she did not remember that she had dreamed at all.

I write that this appearance of Aslan *seems* like a vision, and narrator labels it a "dream" more than once. Yet to Jill it also feels real and visceral, impacting many of her senses. It takes place in the same room in the same conditions as when she went to sleep: with a fire in the fireplace and the toy horse nearby. She not only has a powerful sense of smell, but she can feel the lion's lips and breath. The breath, of course, is an important part: the pointer to the Holy Spirit if indeed the premise of this book is right.

It is after Aslan breathes on Jill that—the following morning—several things happen. We begin to see several changes in Jill. One is that she sleeps really well: fifteen hours, she guesses. She awakes feeling refreshed and cheerful, which is a wonderful gift after many days and weeks of travel and harsh conditions. Was the good night's sleep a gift of Aslan and a result of Aslan's breath? Though the narrator doesn't explicitly say it is, it has always seemed the case to me: that Jill's peaceful sleep in the midst of an anxious time was a gift. Psalm 127 (attributed to Solomon) tells us that God "grants sleep to those he loves." This is not the only place in Scripture that we read of rest and refreshment as gifts from God at times we need them. The start of the more famous Psalm 23 conveys this message beautifully. Jill and her two companions also seem mysteriously prompted to look outside, and in doing so they clearly see one of the signs that Aslan had told her to look for. Jill's thoughts turn from the food and material comfort in the House of Harfang (which had distracted her from her quest) to the words of Aslan: the signs she was supposed to be repeating but had forgotten to repeat. And then, she is led to confession and repentance. That repentance is more than mere feelings of guilt; it prompts an active effort on the part of Jill and her two companions to obey Aslan: to start considering how to follow the signs, even though they know it will be difficult.

Sleep. A recognition of signs (or words) from Aslan. Repentance. And then obedience. All these follow the appearance of Aslan and his breath on Jill.

MORE CONFIRMATION, AND
A TROUBLESOME SCENE

We have already seen how many of the observations from the previous
three Narnia stories—observations about Aslan's breath as a pointer to the
Holy Spirit, and his kiss as a spiritual anointing—can also be found in *The
Silver Chair*. When we come to the end of the quest, we find two more significant references to Aslan's breath and kiss, both in Chapter 16, "The Healing
of Harms." The first happens while Jill and Eustace are still in Narnia. They
have succeeded in their quest with the help of Aslan, but there is no celebration. They have been separated from Rilian who was reunited with his father
Caspian only to see him die very shortly after his return. Thus, though the quest
ends in success, it also ends with sadness and loss—something Lewis himself
experienced serving in World War I. This is the only Narnia story in which
characters from our world are eager rather than sad to leave Narnia at the end
of their adventure. "I wish I were home," Jill says after watching Caspian's death
from afar. Eustace nods his agreement. The words are barely out of Jill's mouth
when Aslan appears behind them. Immediately, Jill remembers her failures on
the quest. Overwhelmed with guilt at all the thing she did wrong, she wants to
say, "I'm sorry," but she can't even speak.

The narrator tells us, "Then the Lion drew them towards him with his eyes,
and bent down and touched their pale faces with his tongue, and said: 'Think of
that no more. I will not always be scolding. You have done the work for which I
sent you into Narnia.'" The touch of his tongue can again be a symbol of anointing, though at this point in the story there is no task for which Aslan would be
anointing Jill and we read no explicit reference *yet* to his breath. I would like
to read Aslan's forgiveness in this scene: something of his merciful character.
Forgiveness is not explicitly mentioned, though Aslan's words ("Think of that
no more") certainly hint at forgiveness and of putting Jill's failures behind her
where they need not be brought up again, even as he did with Edmund in *The
Lion, the Witch and the Wardrobe*. There is also a sense of the master's "Well
done, good and faithful servant" that we read about in Jesus' parable about the
bags of gold (in Matthew 25:21).

What is also interesting to me is that I've never had the impression in any of the Narnia stories that Aslan scolds frequently. Although he does at times correct or rebuke, that correction is done in love and with gentleness and comfort mixed in. Perhaps, because of her feelings of guilt and because she has not come to know Aslan as well as (for example) Lucy has, Jill has the *impression* of being constantly scolded. A central part of the good news of the gospel is that those who follow Christ are forgiven. Satan, the evil one, who is known as the accuser (as well as the deceiver and the devourer), seeks to fill us with guilt and shame. The Holy Spirit helps us experience the truth that we are forgiven: that we need think no more of our past sins.

What we see after Aslan's kiss may be Jill's understanding of that forgiveness. What we read is that her voice is freed up; she is able to speak with Aslan. She repeats to him her desire to go home. It is a prayer, of sorts: an honesty about what she has been feeling and thinking—an honesty that disciples of Christ are called to, and which should be part of any and all prayer. Perhaps it is the work of Aslan's kiss that gives her the freedom to be honest with him in her request. Aslan answers that prayer.

> "Yes. I have come to bring you Home," said Aslan. Then he opened his mouth and blew.... and the wild breath of Aslan blew away the ship and the dead King and the castle and the snow and the winter sky. For all these things floated off into the air like wreaths of smoke, and suddenly they were standing in a great brightness of mid-summer sunshine, on smooth turf, among mighty trees, and beside a fair, fresh stream. Then they saw that they were once more on the Mountain of Aslan.

Here, not long after Aslan's kiss, we get his breath. Again, Jill and Eustace are transported miraculously across the sea, though this time they travel in the opposite direction and the movement is nearly instantaneous. There is no sense of travel: they are in one place, and then they are in another. It is more like how I imagined Philip's miraculous journey. We also read (for the first time) Aslan's breath described as "wild." Numerous times in the books we have read that Aslan is not a tame lion. Now we read that his breath (though gentle and comforting) is not tame either. Aslan and Aslan's breath have the same character.

And there is still one more reference to Aslan's kiss and his breath in this final chapter—though in the opposite order as previous pairings of the two actions. As Jill and Eustace prepare to return to their own world and to the awful Experimental School they have been suffering in, they stand in the gap in the wall with Aslan and Caspian briefly joining them. "Aslan turned to Jill and Eustace and breathed upon them and touched their foreheads with his tongue." Here, as they are about to take part in another task that Aslan has given them— one in their own world, which is also our world and that of the author C.S. Lewis—we read yet again of Aslan's breath and anointing kiss. And just a little later in the same long paragraph describing what happens at the Experimental House, we read that "the strength of Aslan [was] in them."

I confess I find this a disturbing scene. I am not at peace with it. Eustace and Jill, with the help of Caspian, enter the school and with the flats of their swords and a switch they proceed to overcome and beat the gang of bullies and send them running. There are few scenes in Lewis' writing that bother me in the sense that I think he got it wrong (from a moral or spiritual viewpoint), but this is one. Not that I didn't enjoy it when I read it. Indeed, it was quite satisfying. I imagined some of the bullies I used to deal with at my school and in my neigh- borhood—kids who would knock the books out of my hand or punch me in the stomach on my way home from school for no other reason (that I could discern) other than to be mean and prove that they could. Lewis was likely playing out his imaginative fantasies from his own awful boarding school experience. It's an appealing scenario. All too sadly, I am easily drawn to violence like this as a solution to problems. People cheer at the movies in which the heroes beat up on the bad guys at the end. I suspect many Christian readers of *The Silver Chair* imagine scenes like this: solving problems with God-ordained strength and vi- olence. It's the stuff of dreams, isn't it? It may be that this scene has even helped provoke those sorts of ideas and actions among Christ's followers.

My problem is that it doesn't seem Christ-like. It doesn't fit the description we have of Jesus in the New Testament—the image that his followers are called to imitate. The teachings and examples of the Gospels are more along the lines of turning the other cheek and rejoicing when we suffer unjustly. In Jesus' day, the Roman occupiers oppressed the conquered Jews, yet never did Christ help the Jews beat off the Romans with swords and switches—though he certainly had the power to have done so, and had followers who hoped he would. Christians often point to Jesus overturning the tables of the money changers that we read about in Matthew 21 and Mark 11. John 2:15 even mentions that Jesus used a whip of cords in this scene. But Jesus did not do that in a secular setting to punish unbelieving oppressors who mistreated his disciples. He did it in a religious building where the religious leaders had set up a system to profit from the worship of God.

Of course, many readers of this book will disagree with me on this point. Whether we agree or disagree with the particular application Lewis illustrates in this passage, the imagery is still a twofold pointer to Holy Spirit: Aslan's kiss upon the foreheads as an anointing, and his breath as a sending of the Holy Spirit. And shortly after this, the narrator tells us that Aslan's strength was in them. Not Aslan physically, but rather the power of his Spirit, imparted by kiss and breath.

When I first paid attention to Aslan's kiss in *The Lion, the Witch and the Wardrobe*—described only as a lick—I thought something like the following: *This could be a symbol of anointing; it seems to fit well.*

But maybe I'm reading into it more than I should, forcing into the texts something that simply isn't there—it could also just be a warm wet tongue. Now as I look closely at this passage, those doubts have evaporated. Aslan's kiss seems so clearly to be something holy—not merely holy in terms of affection (though it is that, too), but holy in terms of preparation and blessing for a particular task. And like so many examples of anointing in the Bible, it is followed by the empowering presence of the Holy Spirit. The symbolism, along with Aslan's breath, points the reader toward the Holy Spirit. The Third Person of the Trinity is very much present in the Chronicles of Narnia. This book could easily have been titled *The Breath and Kiss of the Lion.*

V

THE HORSE AND HIS BOY

Gentleness and Comfort[9]

Shasta is alone on mountain pass somewhere between Archenland and Narnia, in the cold, misty, dark, with icy winds blowing upon him. And then he finds he is not as alone as he thought, and perhaps not alone as he would have liked—despite his earlier desire for companionship. "Someone or somebody was walking beside him" (Chapter 11).

Aslan pops up all over the place in *The Horse and His Boy*. He seems to be everywhere, even two places at the same time. However, the characters *in* the story often don't know when Aslan is with them, or they don't understand what he was doing until later. And unlike in *The Lion, the Witch and the Wardrobe* (where he personally battles the witch) or *Prince Caspian* (where he calls on Bacchus to destroy Beruna Bridge and awakens the dryads who later join the battle), Aslan does not take part in the battle at Anvard near the end of the story—at least not in any visible or physical way. Thus, despite all the times Aslan is present in the story (unseen or unrecognized), there are only three scenes in which he makes himself known and converses with any of the characters.

---

9   Some of the ideas in this chapter pertaining to gentleness were presented in an essay "A Welcome-Unwelcome Traveler in Narnia" by Matthew Dickerson, in *A Radiant Birth: Advent Readings for a Bright Season*, ed. Leslie Leyland Fields and Paul J. Willis (Downers Grove: Intervarsity Press, 2013).

The first and longest of those three instances is the scene on the mountain pass (in the chapter "An Unwelcome Fellow Traveler") in which he is the "someone or somebody" who walks alongside Shasta. The second is his visit to the home of the Hermit of the Southern March where he speaks with Bree, Hwin, and Aravis. The third and last is his appearance at Anvard in Archenland (after the battle), where he speaks to Rabadash and pronounces the doom of the Calormene prince. Those three scenes provide our only direct opportunities to explore Lewis's portrayal of Aslan in this book, and the last one makes no mention of Aslan's breath or his kiss, so we are left with only two to explore.

In the scene at Anvard, we read of Aslan kissing the horse Hwin and speaking with her. "'Dearest daughter,' said Aslan, planting a lion's kiss on her twitching, velvet nose, 'I knew you would not be long in coming to me. Joy shall be yours'" (Chapter 14). These last words are a wonderful blessing bestowed on the humble horse: the blessing of joy. It is also an affirmation of a faithful horse: one who, though she feared he might eat her, was still drawn to the beauty of Aslan—and also, I think, to his goodness and holiness—saying, "I'd sooner be eaten by you than fed by anyone else." Thus, she chooses to approach him even when her companions hang back.

Christians rightly understand joy to be a spiritual state that is deep and lasting (as opposed to pleasure, which is a state of the body and is often fleeting). As a spiritual state, joy relates both to our spirits and to the Holy Spirit. In Galatians 5:22 (a passage we will return to later in this chapter), Paul describes joy (as well as peace) as fruit of the Holy Spirit. And Jesus, in a long discourse with his disciples (John 14:25–16:33) when he promises "the Advocate, the Holy Spirit," makes multiple references to both the peace and the joy his disciples will have. Thus, in biblical terms we could understand Aslan's blessing on Hwin as a promise of the Spirit's presence in her life. His words at least hint at this. Noting that this kiss precedes that blessing, I think it is fair to the author and the text to put the kiss in the category with earlier references as a spiritual act: a pointer or symbol of anointing. But this is also a short interaction, with no mention of Aslan's breath. This scene at the hermitage is beautiful, but with respect to Aslan's breath and the Holy Spirit I have little else to say about it that does not stretch the imagery beyond what it seems to bear on its own.

That leaves us with only a single passage in *The Horse and His Boy* with overt imagery of the Holy Spirit: a passage that references both Aslan's breath (many times) and also his kiss. Fortunately, it is a long scene, and a powerful one. It is also my favorite scene in all the Chronicles of Narnia.

TEACHING LEWIS, AND THE APPEAL OF ASLAN

On numerous occasions I have taught classes on C.S. Lewis at Middlebury College, a private, secular, liberal arts college in Vermont where I have been on the faculty for more than three decades. Most of these classes have been writing-intensive seminars for first year students, with an enrollment of fifteen. Although we explore some of Lewis's other works, reading through and discussing the Chronicles of Narnia is always a central aspect of the class. Since Middlebury is a secular institution in one of the least religious states in the country, few students in my classes have openly identified as Christians. In a typical year, I might have one to three students who acknowledge any sort of church background or publicly identify with the Christian faith. Most of the students have read *The Lion, the Witch and the Wardrobe* and perhaps some other books from the Chronicles of Narnia. Some have only seen the Narnia films and not read the books. Few have read any of Lewis's works of apologetics or his essays on Christian faith, and thus most know nothing about his religious background. I try to make the class welcoming and engaging for all the students without any assumptions of biblical knowledge (or biblical interest).

Several years ago at the end of one semester I asked my students, partly out of curiosity, which portrayal of Aslan they found most personally compelling or appealing, or which scene (if any) most drew them. The answers I most expected were either the sacrifice at the Stone Table and the subsequent resurrection, or the creation of Narnia in *The Magician's Nephew,* or some other dramatic demonstration of his power. Or perhaps the un-dragoning of Eustace. To my surprise, the vast majority of my students mentioned the scene in *The Horse and His Boy* when Aslan appears as an "Unwelcome Fellow Traveler" and walks alongside Shasta through the mountain pass between Archenland and Narnia. I repeated the question to my class the following year and received the same answer from almost the entire class.

In hindsight, I shouldn't have been surprised. It is my own favorite scene also. C.S. Lewis communicates something both compelling and profound about Aslan in this scene, and my students' response also tells me something about what draws people to Christ. (Hint: It is not messages of hellfire and brimstone, but instead God's kindness and gentleness, which Romans 2:4 tells us leads to repentance.) Aslan's walk with Shasta also contains what to me are the most moving and significant references to Aslan's breath—and thus, if I am correct about Lewis's imagery, to the Holy Spirit. This also makes it my favorite of all the passages I get to write about in this book, and the one whose applications to my own life are most meaningful. It is a passage about human sorrow, but it is also a passage that beautifully points both to the gentleness of Jesus and the comfort of the Holy Spirit.

Before we turn to this one passage in *The Horse and His Boy,* let us consider an important biblical teaching related to the Holy Spirit that can help us understand Lewis's portrayal of Aslan and his imagery of Aslan's breath (and Aslan's kiss)—even as Lewis's imaginative portrayal might deepen our grasp of that biblical teaching and inspire us to follow it.

GENTLENESS AND THE HOLY SPIRIT

Galatians 5:22–23 tells us that the fruit the Holy Spirit bears through his transforming and renewing work in the lives of those who follow Christ includes gentleness. "But the fruit of the Spirit is love, joy, peace, forbearance, kindness, goodness, faithfulness, gentleness and self-control. Against such things there is no law." This reference to gentleness is only a starting point. Gentleness is an important and oft-addressed topic in several New Testament books. It is important enough that the New Testament authors make use of several different Greek words that carry meanings related to gentleness.

Epiekēs is often translated as "gentle" but may also be rendered as "fair," "moderate," "equitable," "forbearing," "mild," or "lenient." Paul uses this word in 1 Timothy 3:3, Philippians 4:5, and Titus 3:2, and uses a noun form in 2 Corinthians 10:1. James uses the word in James 3:17. For both writers, the word provides a description or exhortation for how a disciple of Christ *ought* to live, with different translators choosing a variety of the words given above—including gentleness—to render it. *Épios* can also be translated as "gentle" or "mild," and is found in 1 Thessalonians 2:7, 2 Timothy 2:24, and 2 Cor 11:13, 20—again in descriptions for how followers of Christ *ought* to live.

The adjective *chréstos* and the related noun *chréstotés* are most often translated as "kind" and "kindness" respectively, but they also carry a sense of gentleness. Thus in Galatians 5:22, KJV translates *chréstotés* as "gentleness" (though the NIV uses "kindness"). Paul is fond of the word *chréstotés* and repeatedly encourages this *gentleness-as-kindness* among believers in several epistles including 2 Corinthians 6:6, Ephesians 2:7, Colossians 3:12, and Titus 3:4 as well as in the Galatians 5:22 passage describing the fruit of the spirit.

Another New Testament Greek adjective *praüs* is also usually translated as "gentle," "mild," or "meek." Matthew uses *praüs* three times in his Gospel account, either to describe Jesus or to convey Jesus' teachings. He uses the word in 21:5 as a translation of a passage from Zechariah 9:9 which is a prophetic description of Jesus entering Jerusalem on Palm Sunday: "Say to Daughter Zion, 'See, your king comes to you, gentle and riding on a donkey, and on a colt, the foal of a donkey.'" Matthew also uses *praüs* to render the teachings of Jesus about himself in a passage in which the NIV also translates the word as gentle: "Take my yoke upon you and learn from me, for I am gentle and humble in heart, and you will find rest for your souls" (Matthew 11:29). Perhaps the most famous use of *praüs* is in Matthew 5:5 in the Sermon on the Mount. Here the NIV (keeping with the older and more famous KJV choice)

uses "meek" rather than "gentle": "Blessed are the meek, for they will inherit the earth." However, the NAS opts for "gentle" for this beatitude.

The noun form of *praüs* is *praütés*, often translated as "meekness" or "gentleness." Paul uses *praütés* in Ephesians 4:2 (where NIV, NAS, and NRSV all translate the word as "gentleness") and in Colossians 3:12 (where it is rendered as "gentleness" in NIV and NAS and as "meekness" in NRSV). James uses a version of this word in James 3:13 along with *sophias* (the possessive form of the word for wisdom) to describe true wisdom. The NIV translates James's phrase as "humility that comes from wisdom"; the RSV translates it as "meekness of wisdom"; the NAS translates it as "gentleness of wisdom"; and the NRSV goes with "gentleness born of wisdom."

And this brings us back to the fruit of the Holy Spirit. Paul also uses the word *praütés* (along with *chréstotés*) in Galatians 5:22–23. Thus, two of the nine words describing the fruit of the Spirit carry a connotation of gentleness. Given the meanings of those words and the different translations of that passage, it would be reasonable to read Galatians 5:22 as: "But the fruit of the Spirit is love, joy, peace, forbearance, *gentleness-as-kindness*, goodness, faithfulness, *gentleness-as-meekness* and self-control." Gentleness is clearly an important aspect of the work (or fruit) of the Holy Spirit in the lives of Christ's followers. This should not be surprising, because it is an important element of the character of Christ, as well as a trait that Christ's followers are called to imitate.

This is all worth pointing out because our modern culture does not hold gentleness in high esteem. To state the obvious, gentleness is severely lacking on social media and in public discourse. How often do we (or others we observe) respond with harshness or ridicule when somebody writes something we (or they) disagree with? Think of the constant barrage of memes that fly around Facebook with the point of belittling another group or belief. Or consider how many television and radio shows feature characters who delight in being mean or harsh: who regularly demean and insult others, or who get ahead by cutting others down. This includes dramas, so- called "reality" shows, sports talk shows, and sitcoms. Even cooking shows feature chefs belittling contestants. Why? Ratings of political and sports talk shows (both radio and television) are presumably bolstered by hosts harshly putting people down. Demeaning bosses who boast in the power to fire people (and seem to delight in ruining the careers of others) become global celebrities by doing so. These harsh characters are portrayed as rich, powerful, and successful. Meanness is glorified and put forth as a model, while kindness and gentleness are devalued and seen as week.

We could jump from these celebrities to the world of so-called superheroes. We live in a culture entertained by figures from Marvel and DC Comics. Some of the most successful and influential films of the past two decades have been superhero films. And here the conversation hits close to home for me. My three adult sons grew up with and continue to watch superhero movies and televisions shows which I have happily watched with them: Iron Man, Thor, Hulk, Daredevil, Doctor Strange, Wolverine, Superman, Aquaman, Wonder Woman, and Batman to name just a few. These superheroes win their battles by being stronger, faster, more powerful, and sometimes smarter or by devising and employing better gadgets and weapons than their enemies. Although a few of them—Spiderman and Captain America come to mind—have occasional moments that approach gentleness (at least in comparison with other heroes in their entourage), very few so-called superheroes are icons of gentleness. Indeed, if you consider character descriptions that are opposites of gentle—bullying, authoritarian, rude, mean, bossy, pushy, demanding, manipulative, harsh, callous—you may have a good description of many popular icons, celebrities, and heroes of the day. Our culture devalues and even disdains gentleness.

What makes this particularly sad is that such *ungentleness* is often seen, modeled, and even defended in the church. Some pastors and influential leaders and figures in the Christian church argue that the realities of our modern era require a strong, harsh approach to match that of the world, and that we must abandon gentleness to win our battles—often the so-called "culture wars." *Our situation is desperate,* they say. *The church (or our value system) is under attack. We cannot afford to be gentle.* They preach the same message that J.R.R. Tolkien's character Denethor preached to his son Faramir (in *The Return of the King*): "Ever your desire is to appear lordly and generous as a king of old, gracious, gentle. That may well befit one of high race, if he sits in power and peace. But in desperate hours gentleness may be repaid with death" (V/iv).

But nowhere in the teachings or example of Jesus, or of his apostles who gave us the Scriptures, do we read the message that gentleness is only to be practiced when it is convenient and easy, when things are going our way, or when gentleness is effective at getting what we want. We are called to imitate Christ *all* the time, even when things *seem* desperate (from our limited human perspective). Gentleness is Christ-like. If we want to imitate Christ—which is what the Holy Spirit empowers us to do—we should seek to grow in gentleness and to practice gentleness. Which is why Faramir's response to his father has always struck me as one of the most moving and powerful lines in *The Lord of the Rings* and one which we need to see modeled more often in the church. To his father's statement that "gentleness may be repaid with death," Faramir responds simply, "So be it" (V/iv).

We need more heroes like Faramir to inspire our imagination and to be powerful witnesses to the world. For the harsher the world is, the more that Christ-like gentleness will stand out in contrast. I believe people are eager for gentleness, and that this is why the scene with Aslan and Shasta has been so appealing to my students. Indeed, that this passage draws my students toward Aslan is, I believe, a wonderful illustration of what Paul writes about in Romans 2:4: "Or do you show contempt for the riches of his kindness, forbearance and patience, not realizing that God's kindness is intended to lead you to repentance?"

THE GENTLENESS OF AN UNWELCOME FELLOW TRAVELER

This brings us back to Chapter 11 of *The Horse and His Boy* where Shasta finds himself all alone on a mountain pass between Archenland and Narnia— or, rather, where he finds that he is *not* all alone. The scene begins with Shasta feeling sorry for himself and crying, only to have his self-pity interrupted by his awareness of a presence.

> What put a stop to all this was a sudden fright. Shasta discovered that someone or somebody was walking beside him. It was pitch dark and he could see nothing. And the Thing (or Person) was going so quietly that he could hardly hear any footfalls. What he could hear was breathing. His invisible companion seemed to breathe on a very large scale, and Shasta got the impression that it was a very large creature. And he had come to

notice this breathing so gradually that he had really no idea how long it had been there. It was a horrible shock.

Note that we have not just one but three references in three successive sentences to the breath of the creature beside him. The breath of the giant is clearly important. Of course, readers—even if they haven't guessed who that giant is by the end of this paragraph—learn by the end of the chapter that it is Aslan. Aslan is present with Shasta. His presence is known through his breath (the one thing Shasta "could hear"), even as Christ is present with and known to his followers in the person of the Holy Spirit. Lewis also emphasizes that Shasta's companion is invisible to him. Thus, the breath is described as a palpable way for Shasta to experience what at the time cannot be seen. Consider also the narrator's description that the breathing was sensed by Shasta "on a very large scale." The breath fills space. It is all around him, surrounding and encompassing him (much like Jill's experience when she rode on that breath). It is everywhere. As an image of the Holy Spirit, this is also a fitting description.

The scene continues. Shasta stops crying. He is terrified. For a moment, the terror is more powerful than the sorrow. Time passes, and we read:

> The Thing (unless it was a Person) went on beside him so very quietly that Shasta began to hope he had only imagined it. But just as he was becoming quite sure of it, there suddenly came a deep, rich sigh out of the darkness beside him. That couldn't be imagination! Anyway, he had felt the hot breath of that sigh on his chilly left hand.

The Thing is indeed a person: the person of Aslan. Here we have yet another mention of Aslan's breath. Or rather three mentions, counting two mentions of the sigh—the "deep, rich sigh" that comes out of the darkness. For a sigh is but an audible breath. And in the next paragraph we get a seventh reference to Aslan's breath: "So [Shasta] went on at a walking pace and the unseen companion walked and breathed beside him." Again, it is the *breath* of Aslan by which Shasta is aware of the *presence* of Aslan (though he does not yet know Aslan by name). Aslan's breath is such a central image here that readers should not miss it. It is also a breath or spirit that warms Shasta when he is cold: a spirit of comfort and of life.

When I think of a sigh, which is a sort of wordless expression, I cannot help but think of another wordless expression attributed the Holy Spirit in Romans 8:26. The NIV uses the noun *groans* to translates this passage: "In the same way, the Spirit helps us in our weakness. We do not know what we ought to pray for, but the Spirit himself intercedes for us through wordless groans." Although most translations opt for *groans*, the NRSV uses *sighs:* "Likewise the Spirit helps us in our weakness; for we do not know how to pray as we ought, but that very Spirit intercedes with sighs too deep for words." Both translations reference the wordlessness of the expression. Lewis's description of Aslan's wordless sigh echoes Paul's description of the Holy Spirit.

What of it? This does far more than simply support the understanding of Aslan's breath as an image of or pointer toward the Holy Spirit. It imaginatively reveals something very important that followers of Christ should take to heart. Shasta is lonely. He has lived a life of loneliness. The book begins with his loneliness (and maltreatment) in the house of Arsheesh, and in this scene he is separated from his three new companions—he is alone once more. He longs for somebody to talk with. Prayer is both the greatest conversation, and the most intimate one. It is our ongoing conversation with God, through his Holy Spirit. Though Shasta has never met Aslan, and has no language for prayer, his deepest longing is for the conversation and relationship that is satisfied only by the Creator himself. He knows no Name to which he can speak. He may be terrified to speak to the great Presence beside him. Perhaps he does not even know what to say. Yet Aslan is waiting for him. In his first words to Shasta, Aslan introduces himself as "One who has waited long for you to speak." The wordless sigh that is the breath of Aslan is the start of that conversation. It is like the Holy Spirit reaching out to those who do not (yet) believe, calling them into relationship—for God desires all to be in relationship with him. He created us for that relationship.

When I read that scene, I also think of what I have read of Lewis's own conversion to Christianity: a conversion Lewis himself describes as involving terror, but also as an experience of God speaking to him through his own longing and sense of loss. (Like his character Shasta, Lewis had also lost his mother at a young age.) In Chapter 14 of his autobiographical book *Surprised by Joy,* Lewis describes the final scene of his own coming into faith in God:

> You must picture me alone in that room at Magdalen, night after night, feeling, whenever my mind lifted even for a second from my work, the steady, unrelenting approach of Him whom I so earnestly desired not to meet. That which I greatly feared had at last come upon me. In the Trinity Term of 1929 I gave in, and admitted that God was God, and knelt and prayed: perhaps, that night, the most dejected and reluctant convert in all England.

THE HOLY SPIRIT AS COMFORTER

It is after Aslan's invitation for Shasta to speak—and after several of Aslan's breaths and his poignant sighs—that we come to the heart of Shasta's prayer. It is a very important prayer: a prayer that is a beautiful conversation that, more than any other passage in the Chronicles of Narnia, brings tears quickly to my eyes. Even reading it now, and typing the words out on my screen, my eyes grow damp. It is also a prayer that many followers of Christ could learn much from.

> "I can't see you at all," said Shasta, after staring very hard. Then (for an even more terrible idea had come into his head) he said, almost in a scream, "You're not—not something dead, are you? Oh please—please do go away. What harm have I ever done you? Oh, I am the unluckiest person in the whole world."
> Once more he felt the warm breath of the Thing on his hand and face.
> "There," it said, "that is not the breath of a ghost. Tell me your sorrows."
> Shasta was a little reassured by the breath.

I suspect many readers can relate to Shasta's initial problem: he is speaking with a being whom he cannot see. It is hard to speak with one we cannot see. It can be hard to pray to a God we cannot see. And when Shasta thinks for a moment that he might be speaking with a ghost, he is also in good company; some of Jesus' disciples thought the same about Jesus when they saw him walking across the water (Matthew 14:26, Mark 6:49) and again later after the resurrection (Luke 24:37–39). And Aslan, too, had once been dead. Perhaps readers who have a fear of ghosts or giants can sympathize with Shasta for wanting Aslan to go away—for wanting to be left alone.

Much could be said about the start of this prayer-that-is-a-conversation or conversation-that- is-a-prayer. We might return to another word that also describes the impact of Aslan's breath. Earlier in the chapter, we considered the trait of gentleness and the related idea of kindness. Something that captures both of those is *comfort*. Again, not the "comfort" that refers to material possessions which can buffer us from physical pain (as when we talk about somebody having a comfortable home or a comfortable life), but the sort of comfort we offer to somebody who is grieving. I speak here of the sort of comfort Paul had in mind when he wrote to the church in Corinth, "Praise be to the God and Father of our Lord Jesus Christ, the Father of compassion and the God of all comfort, who comforts us in all our troubles, so that we can comfort those in any trouble with the comfort we ourselves receive from God" (2 Corinthians 1:3–4). This is the sort of comfort that is often best expressed through listening or just through our presence. When Job is suffering, his three friends Eliphaz, Bildad, and Zophar come to him and are said to "sympathize with him and comfort him." They do this simply by being with him, sitting on the ground with him for several days and seven nights without saying a word "because they saw how great his suffering was" (Job 2:13). This is a wonderful response. Sadly, these same three later cease to be Job's comforters and become instead his accusers, but their initial actions give an indication of what true comfort can look like.

As for how God comforts his people, we can consider again that Jesus spoke of the Holy Spirit as the *parekletos* (John 14:16, 26)—a word often translated as "Helper" or "Advocate" but also sometimes translated as "Comforter." The Holy Spirit comes to us as a comforter. And in this conversation between Aslan and Shasta, Lewis gives us an imaginative picture of what the comfort of the Holy Spirit is like. When Shasta comes near to screaming—when he is at his most intense moment of fear and anxiety—Aslan's response is not one of correction or rational explanation (or scolding), but of comfort: a warm breath on Shasta's hand. "There," Aslan says after breathing yet again on Shasta, as though the breath itself were the important thing, and not any word of explanation. And, indeed, the narrator tells us not that Shasta was reassured by any words, but rather that "Shasta was a little reassured *by the breath*" [emphasis added]. When Shasta needs comfort, Aslan breathes on him and reassures him. Aslan's breath is comfort, even as the Holy Spirit is the Comforter.

It is that last statement of Shasta's above— "Oh, I am the unluckiest person in the whole world"—followed by Aslan's response that begins the conversation in earnest. It would be tempting to hear Shasta's words merely as a complaint: as a boy whining because things aren't going his way. I suppose that's at least partly an accurate description. Yet it is also an honest expression of his feelings and a reflection of real loss and sorrow that he has experienced. Shasta is talking with Aslan. He is opening his heart to the Great Lion. And Aslan is listening. Perhaps the most powerful words in the Chronicles of Narnia—the words spoken by Aslan that are most moving at least to me, and I believe also to many of my former students who know little of Jesus and yet I'm sure have longed for what he offers them—are Aslan's words of invitation: "Tell me your sorrows."

In the earlier section I wrote about the gentleness and kindness that the Holy Spirit seeks to build in our charac- ter. It is a gentleness and kindness that is Christlike. Or, we might also note, a gentleness that is Aslan-like. It is also a gentleness at the core of the comfort we seek—and that we see in this scene. Aslan does not chastise Shasta for whining. He does not silence him or belittle him or tell simply him to toughen him or grow up. He does not say in the idiom of the 2010 decade, "Don't be a snowflake!" Instead, Aslan listens. More than merely listening, he encourages Shasta to speak. Very specifically, he invites Shasta to express his sorrows. And Shasta does. He pours out his life story with all the grief and heartache and loss: the "heat and thirst" and the times we have been in the desert. Oh, that we were all so free to speak to our Savior in such a way!

And yet we are. If only we would allow ourselves that honesty. He will listen to us. The Holy Spirit will be right alongside us sighing with us.

After listening to Shasta share his sorrows, Aslan does answer him in a way. He does not deny or diminish Shasta's sorrow and grief. Shasta's life has had a large share of grief. He was without parents and mistreated by his foster father Arsheesh. He has never had friends. At the very moment when he reaches the house of the Hermit of the Southern March and thinks things might get better, he must leave even his momentary refuge. He finds safety and welcome in the company of Anvard only to be lost yet again. Though we live in a world full of God-created beauty, a world with much that can lead to delight, it is also a sinful world full of loss, grief, hardship, and suffering: a world of divorce and death, cancer and Covid, racism and rage, floods and fires and wars, betrayal and broken homes. Aslan affirms the reality of sorrow in a difficult world.

Yet while he doesn't deny the sorrow, and even invites Shasta to share it, the one important thing Aslan does point out is that Shasta was never alone. Aslan was with him all along, not only protecting and directing him but also comforting him ("I was the cat who comforted you among the houses of the dead," he tells Shasta), even as we today—those who follow Christ—have the promise that God will never leave us or forsake us. The Holy Spirit is with us always. Even to the ends of the earth! Aslan reveals that he has been Shasta's rescuer and protector: his savior, as it were. In that sense, Shasta was wrong about one thing: he was not unlucky. That is the only correction that Aslan makes. It was Shasta's openness and honesty in "prayer" about his own grief that leads to this deeper relationship.

A TRIUNE GOD REVEALED

This idea of honesty in conversation with Aslan (and with God), invited by Aslan (and by God)—including sharing our sorrows—leads to a few final thoughts for this chapter. If you were paying close attention to that previous passage, you noticed two more mentions of Aslan's breath, bringing the total to nine (counting the two mentions of a sigh) in a relatively short scene. Does it leave any doubt that this breath is an important symbol? And if you read just a little farther to the end of the scene, you will see the resulting impact on Shasta of Aslan's presence, Aslan's breath, and Aslan's words. For the second time in the dialogue Shasta asks "Who are you?" This time, Aslan gives a different answer.

> "Myself," said the Voice, very deep and low so that the earth shook: and again "Myself," loud and clear and gay: and then the third time "Myself," whispered so softly you could hardly hear it, and yet it seemed to come from all round you as if the leaves rustled with it.
>
> Shasta was no longer afraid that the Voice belonged to something that would eat him, nor that it was the voice of a ghost. But a new and different sort of trembling came over him. Yet he felt glad too.

The soft whisper that Aslan ends with is yet another pointer to his gentleness, very much like the way God revealed himself to Elijah on Mount Horeb through a "gentle whisper" (1 Kings 19:11–12). Sometimes Christians want to appear to the world like a raging wind that tears mountains apart and shatters rocks, or like an earthquake or fire—something powerful that forces the enemy into submission—but God was not in the rock-shattering wind, the earthquake, or the fire on Mount Horeb. He was in the gentle whisper. Those who want to *rule* the world in their own way may seek the power of the earthquake and fire (and claim they want to rule for Jesus). But if we want to *reveal* Jesus to the world (rather than trying to rule in his stead), then an approach of Christ-like gentleness would seem to be a much better way. If we want to have a real impact on others, we might also listen to their sorrows, even as we are free to share ours with God. That, at least, seems to be what C.S. Lewis is illustrating.

Who is Aslan? He is himself. He might well have said, "I am that I am," as God did when he revealed himself to Moses at the burning bush (Exodus 3:14). It is a name that speaks not merely to existence but to self-existence. It is a name that transcends any one descriptive or doctrinal statement we might make about *God*. It is also a name, when spoken personally—as Aslan does with Shasta or God does with Moses—that reveals the very presence of the speaker. After Shasta's honesty and vulnerability with him, what Aslan reveals to Shasta through his words and his breath is the most important thing: not merely an abstract truth *about* himself (though he does reveal his own presence in Shasta's history), but himself: the loving, comfortering one who has never—not once—left Shasta alone. It is not enough to know facts about God. We want to be in relationship with God, to know Jesus. The Holy Spirit reveals the Son (not just facts about the Son) even as the Son reveals the Father (and not just doctrinal statements about the Father), because Father, Son, and Holy Spirit are one.

At the end, Shasta is no longer afraid. Or, rather, he is no longer afraid *in the same way*. He is not afraid that Aslan will hurt him. His sorrow has turned to gladness. He has, in a word, been comforted. Sharing his sorrows with Aslan has led to his receiving of comfort. We read that "the night was over at last." That doesn't mean that all of Shasta's griefs have forever passed. But this particular night has.

And then comes the kiss that has so often been associated with his breath: the anointing that comes with the spirit—this time with the added imagery of a perfume that would have been a familiar part of a biblical anointing—and our imagery is complete.

> The High King above all kings stooped towards him. Its mane, and some strange and solemn perfume that hung about the mane, was all around him. It touched his forehead with its tongue. He lifted his face and their eyes met. Then instantly the pale brightness of the mist and the fiery brightness of the Lion rolled themselves together into a swirling glory and gathered themselves up and disappeared.

VI

THE MAGICIAN'S NEPHEW

Breath and Wind at Creation

Although *The Magician's Nephew* describes the creation of Narnia and could therefore, in terms of the chronological history of Narnia, be listed as the first book, it was sixth of seven to be published. Thus, by the time C.S. Lewis wrote this book he had been thinking and writing about Narnia for several years. The geography and history of his created world had grown larger and more fully developed with each successive book, with stories having been set in the seas and islands to the east of Narnia, then the human-inhabited lands to the south (Calormen and Archenland), and then the lands of the giants to the north. My own impression is that the imagery of Aslan's breath and kiss had also steadily become more fully developed leading up to this sixth book.

The Magician's Nephew also takes place prior to the death and resurrection of Aslan. If we were to draw a parallel between Lewis's history of Narnia and the biblical account of God's work in our world, we might think of *The Magician's Nephew* as filling the space of the Old Testament, and more specifically of the Genesis 1–3 account of creation and fall. In the chronology of Narnia, this is long before Aslan's death and resurrection on the Stone Table, and before Aslan's breath comes to rest on the many stone statues in the courtyard of the White Witch—a scene we earlier associated with the day of Pentecost when the Holy Spirit came on all of God's people in a new way. We might therefore expect a different sort of portrayal of Aslan's breath (and the Holy Spirit) in this book than in any of the others except the first half of *The Lion, the Witch and the Wardrobe*.

Yet if we see in these stories a consistent portrayal of biblical themes and theology—as, indeed, I do—we might still expect some pointers to or portrayals of the Holy Spirit even in this pre-resurrection story. For the Spirit of God is mentioned many times in the Bible prior to Pentecost and to Christ's promise of the coming comforter. He is not only mentioned, but he is present and active. There are numerous Old Testament passages describing the Spirit of God coming in power upon a particular person—most often a prophet or an anointed leader of Israel: Moses, Bezalel son of Uri (Exodus 31:2–3), the seventy elders of Israel (Numbers 11:16–17), Balaam, Gideon, Samuel, Saul, David, Elijah, and many others. Earlier in this book, when we first explored Aslan's kiss as a symbol of anointing, we explored a few of these. Similarly, we will see an example in *The Magician's Nephew* of Aslan's breath and anointing kiss upon the book's titular character.

More than that, however, we read all the way back at the start of Genesis (before any humans appeared in the created world) that the *ruach elohim*—the *spirit* or *breath* or *wind* of God—was over the deep at the start of creation. It is with the imagery surrounding the Holy Spirit at the creation of Narnia that we start our exploration of *The Magician's Nephew*.

THE SONG, WIND, AND BREATH OF ASLAN

The account of the creation of Narnia begins in Chapter 8 of *The Magician's Nephew*. There are at least a few aspects of the description worth observing before we get to the first mention of Aslan's breath which does not come until Chapter 9. The creation narrative begins with a voice, which those who have read the series in order of publication will quickly recognize as Aslan. We hear and later see the scene unfold through the perspective of the eponymous character Digory.

> A voice had begun to sing. It was very far away and Digory found it hard to decide from what direction it was coming. Sometimes it seemed to come from all directions at once. Sometimes he almost thought it was coming out of the earth beneath them. Its lower notes were deep enough to be the

voice of the earth herself. There were no words. There was hardly even a tune. But it was, beyond comparison, the most beautiful noise he had ever heard. It was so beautiful he could hardly bear it.

When Aslan appears a few paragraphs later, he is in the incarnate form of a lion. Yet Digory's initial sense of this voice is one of omnipresence: it "seemed to come from all directions at once" and also "out of the earth beneath them." Christians understand God to be omnipresent as well as omnipotent and omniscient. Yet while this is a true description of the fullness of the Trinitarian God—of Father, Son, and Holy Spirit—when Jesus walked the earth in first century Galilee, he had taken on finite mortal flesh and humbled himself to be in one physical place and one moment of time. Thus that description of the voice being "everywhere at once" may sound more familiar with respect to the Holy Spirit than the *incarnate* Son of God. This might already be a suggestion of the presence of the Third Person of the Trinity, or it might be that Aslan has not yet taken the form of a Lion.

It also struck me as I reread this passage that this singing voice at first lacks both words and even a melody. Whether or not Aslan has yet taken bodily form, from Digory's perspective the voice is disembodied, wordless, and tuneless (if not toneless). The voice is indeed much like a breath. Like spirit rather than flesh. The point of this comment is *not* to place the Holy Spirit at creation *without* God the Son. The character (and the readers) soon become aware that Aslan is present in incarnate form as a lion. The point, rather, is that there are hints of the three persons of the triune God fully present, at work, and involved in creation. Although at the start of this chapter I associated *The Magician's Nephew* with the first three chapters of Genesis, in some ways it bears more in common with the creation account in John 1. We have a Voice (or Word) that is with God, and is God, becoming flesh and entering into the world of his making, presenting a more explicit image of God the Son portrayed as both Creator and as part of creation.

A little later, after stars appear and briefly add a celestial chorus, we read, "The Voice on the earth was now louder and more triumphant.... Far away, and down near the horizon, the sky began to turn grey. A light wind, very fresh, began to stir. The sky, in that one place, grew slowly and steadily paler. You could see shapes of hills standing up dark against it. All the time the Voice went on singing." Remember that the words used for spirit in both biblical Hebrew and New Testament Greek can also mean *breath* or *wind*. So far, I have written very little about wind. Wind has certainly been mentioned in the Narnia stories, and it plays a significant role in *The Voyage of the Dawn Treader*—which is not surprisingly since the voyage takes place on the sailing vessel somewhat at the whims of the wind! Yet for the most part when we read of wind in Narnia it really does seem like moving air and nothing more. But keeping in mind the imagery of Genesis 1:2 and the fact that the Voice is still disembodied, here at creation it could well point us to the *ruach elohim* which is either the Spirit of God or the Breath of God or the Wind of God. Or somehow, mysteriously, it is all of the above. On the day of Pentecost, the coming of the Holy Spirit was not only seen in the tongues of flame (Acts 2:3) and then manifested in the speaking of many languages; even before the appearance of the flames, those present heard a "sound like a mighty rushing wind" that "filled the entire house where they were sitting" (Acts 2:2 ESV). It is also interesting, though I'm not sure what to make of it, that "voice" is not initially capitalized, but in this passage it suddenly becomes "the Voice."

As the creation narrative continues, we get another mention of wind. The source of the Voice has by now become visible. "It was a Lion. Huge, shaggy, and bright it stood facing the risen sun. Its mouth was wide open in song and it was about three hundred yards away." The Voice has become flesh and is now within his creation. And then in Chapter 9 we read:

> The Lion was pacing to and fro about that empty land and singing his new song. It was softer and more lilting than the song by which he had called up the stars and the sun; a gentle, rippling music. And as he walked and sang the valley grew green with grass. It spread out from the Lion like a pool. It ran up the sides of the little hills like a wave. In a few minutes it was creeping up the lower slopes of the distant mountains, making that young world every moment softer. The light wind could now be heard ruffling the grass.

Now that the Lion is visible, and the Voice is coming from one particular direction and is both softer and more melodic—clearly now a song, or something that can becalled music: a "gentle, rippling music"—the wind and the Voice of the lion are two separate entities, each making its own sounds. I think of Jesus' words to Nicodemus: "The wind blows wherever it pleases. You hear its sound, but you cannot tell where it comes from or where it is going. So it is with everyone born of the Spirit" (John 3:8).

Only after all this do we get an explicit reference to Aslan's breath. As with many previous examples, Aslan's breath is preceded with something like an anointing kiss. Here the anointing is described as a touch of his nose to the noses of the creatures he will breathe on. And with his touch and breath, Aslan also speaks words that are both a blessing and also an anointing with a purpose.

> And every now and then he would go up to two of them (always two at a time) and touch their noses with his. He would touch two beavers among all the beavers, two leopards among all the leopards, one stag and one deer among all the deer, and leave the rest. Some sorts of animal he passed over altogether. But the pairs which he had touched instantly left their own kinds and followed him. At last he stood still and all the creatures whom he had touched came and stood in a wide circle around him .... The Lion opened his mouth, but no sound came from it; he was breathing out, a long, warm breath; it seemed to sway all the beasts as the wind sways a line of trees. Far overhead from beyond the veil of blue sky which hid them the stars sang again; a pure, cold, difficult music. Then there came a swift flash like fire (but it burnt nobody) either from the sky or from the Lion itself, and every drop of blood tingled in the children's bodies, and the deepest, wildest voice they had ever heard was saying:
>
> "Narnia, Narnia, Narnia, awake. Love. Think. Speak. Be walking trees. Be talking beasts. Be divine waters."

Here we read what may be the most significant mention of Aslan's breath in the Chronicles of Narnia, and one different from the others. It is the breath of Aslan at creation: "a long, warm breath" that is also a wind that "seemed to sway all the beasts." If the earlier imagery of the wind alone was too subtle to make it clear, this imagery associating the wind with the breath of Aslan should be clearer: the Spirit of God is present at creation. God's Holy Spirit is a creative spirit. It is a life-giving spirit, present from all eternity and at the start of time. What we see in this scene, then, appears to be the *ruach elohim*: simultaneously the breath, wind, and spirit of Aslan.

And not only is God's Holy Spirit present, but spirit is imparted to the creatures: a new kind of wind and breath by which they become spiritual beings, capable of loving and receiving love, of knowing Aslan and of being known, of thinking on their own and choosing to follow or not to follow Aslan. It is a mystery too great to understand and nothing I can put into a rational formula, but which Lewis portrays beautifully through story. By God's Holy Spirit, spirit is imparted to us, his image bearers. "The LORD God formed the man of dust from the ground and breathed into his nostrils the breath of life, and the man became a living creature" (Genesis 2:7).

It is also worth noting that Aslan's first (and greatest) command is to love.

COMFORT, STRENGTH, COURAGE, AND THE DIGNITY OF CAUSALITY

We come then to Chapter 12, the one scene in *The Magician's Nephew* explicitly referencing both Aslan's breath and his kiss. The grand creation narrative is complete; the animals have been given speech and spirit; Narnia has been established. It has its first king and queen. Aslan now addresses Digory. He has already drawn from Digory a confession of his culpability in bringing evil to Narnia (we will soon return to this important passage), and now Aslan has a task for him. Digory, who up to that point had been thinking primarily about his mother, hoping for her healing—pondering even trying to bargain with Aslan—concludes he is in no position to make any demands of Aslan. Near to despair, he begins to cry. And wonder of wonders, tears appear also in Aslan's eyes,

> such big, bright tears compared with Digory's own that for a moment he felt as if the Lion must really be sorrier about his Mother than he was himself.
>
> "My son, my son," said Aslan. "I know. Grief is great. Only you and I in this land know that yet." ...
>
> The Lion drew a deep breath, stooped its head even lower and gave

[Digory] a Lion's kiss. And at once Digory felt that new strength and courage had gone into him.

"Dear son," said Aslan, "I will tell you what you must do."

Again, we have both the kiss and the breath. Although the narrator speaks
of Aslan *drawing* a breath rather than breathing out, the reference to a "deep
breath" is still explicit. To breathe is both to breathe in is also to breathe out.
As I read of Aslan stooping over Digory, I imagine Aslan exhaling on Digory
with the deep breath he has just drawn. Then we read the explicit reference to
the kiss, which we have already seen associated with Aslan's breath in several
previous passages. With the breath and kiss of Aslan, we see three things right
away that we have already associated with the Holy Spirit. First is comfort
in grief, much as we saw with Shasta on the pass between Archenland and
Narnia. Aslan does not diminish the reality of Digory's sorrow. He joins him in
that sorrow, shedding his own tears alongside Digory. In this world, loss and
grief are real, and we can bring them to God. We are invited to do so, and we are
reminded of Aslan's invitation to Shasta: "Tell me your sorrows." And even as
the Holy Spirit is described as our Comforter, so too does Aslan's breath bring
comfort. We could certainly say more on this aspect of the passage if we had
not already addressed it in *The Horse and His Boy*.

The second and third impacts of Aslan's kiss and breath on Digory are
also ones we have already seen examples of in previous books: strength and
courage. Yet they are worth mentioning again because they are important. After
the breath, Digory immediately feels that strength and courage have "gone into
him." The impact is palpable. And as the Scriptures tell us, strength and courage (like comfort) are often associated with the Holy Spirit's work in our lives,
empowering God's people to do the work God calls us to do. Comfort. Strength.
Courage. These are all evidence of the Holy Spirit even as they are evident in
those who receive the breath of Aslan.

That brings us to one more important thing we see in this passage, which I
hinted at in the previous section but have not yet explored. Aslan's final words
in that passage are, "I will tell you what you must do." In his essay "The Efficacy
of Prayer," C.S. Lewis uses the phrase "dignity of causality" (which he borrows

from the writings of Pascal) to describe our human volition and agency: that we, God's image-bearers, have been given the gift of freedom that allows us to have a real impact on the world through our actions including even our prayers. Lewis writes in that essay, "Whenever we act at all He lends us that dignity [of causality]. . . . For He seems to do nothing of Himself which He can possibly delegate to His creatures. He commands us to do slowly and blunderingly what He could do perfectly in the twinkling of an eye. He allows us to neglect what He would have us do, or to fail." Given God's sovereign power, this human agency is a mystery, as Lewis goes on to acknowledge: "Perhaps we do not fully realize the problem, so to call it, of enabling finite free wills to co-exist with Omnipotence. It seems to involve at every moment almost a sort of divine abdication. . . . This is how (no light matter) God makes something—indeed, makes gods—out of nothing" (9).

When Aslan breathes on his creatures during the creation account, he gives them spirit and with it the ability to think and love and obey. This also means the ability not to think, or to think with evil intent; the ability to hate rather than love; the ability to disobey. In short, Aslan has given to his creatures the gift of moral agency that comes with spirit and breath. In his book *Christ Plays in Ten Thousand Places,* Eugene Peterson uses similar language of "dignity" to describe the freedom God gave to his human image-bearing creatures that we read about in the Genesis 2 creation account. Peterson writes that we are made of the stuff of the earth but have also been given the breath (or spirit) of life.

> We are not, of course, merely dust. The Lord God breathed into the nostrils of this dust- man who then became a "living being." As the breath of God infuses this form that we humans are, an enormous dignity accumulates around and within us. . . . He deals with us in a more personal, relational way. . . . First, God involves us in a continuation of his creation work. . . . We are put to work, which is to say, we have something useful to do, participating in God's creation under God's direction. (77–78)

Peterson goes on a few paragraphs later to reference the command God gives to his created beings in Genesis 2:16–17: not to eat of the tree of the knowledge of good and evil.

The command announces our capacity for freedom. . . . The command marks the freedom to say yes or no, choose this or that, go here or there, think our own thoughts and sing our own songs. . . . This command, which presumes the freedom to obey or disobey, is the first command given in our Scriptures. It defines us as creatures of freedom: We can decide which road to travel; we are not pre-determined. We have the capacity to say, "Yes, I'll do that," or "No, I don't think I'll do that." (78–79)

Lewis illustrates in the character of Digory (and especially in the scene in which Aslan breathes on him) this two-fold freedom that both allows disobedience and also allows us to participate in God's redemptive work in creation. In the dialogue preceding his breathing on Digory, Aslan questions Digory in such a way as to make clear his moral agency (or we might say moral responsibility and culpability). Like many previous scenes with other characters in the Chronicles of Narnia, Digory wants to describe Jadis's presence in Narnia in the passive voice or to blame other characters. Aslan nudges Digory toward acknowledging his own responsibility. Evil didn't simply come into Narnia; through a series of his free will choices, Digory *brought* evil into Narnia.

Later, after giving Digory the chance to confess, Aslan speaks the truth and makes clear (perhaps as a teaching moment to the other creatures, who have also been given the breath of life and the freedom that comes with it): "Before the new clean world I gave you is seven hours old, a force of evil has already entered it; waked and brought hither by this son of Adam" (Chapter 11). Again, Aslan repeats Digory's moral culpability when he asks him (shortly before breathing on him in Chapter 12), "Are you ready to undo the wrong that you have done to my sweet country of Narnia on the very day of its birth?" But this later reference to Digory's responsibility is also a gift. Digory cannot get rid of all evil in Nania, or the suffering it will cause. That will be up to Aslan who will later pay a steep price to rid Narnia of the White Witch, while the evil as a whole won't be eliminated until the end of time when the world is renewed. Yet even as Digory was given the dignity of causality in choosing to do wrong, he is also given the privilege of taking personal steps to work against the results of sin. By the power of the Holy Spirit, all followers of Christ work to live out God's kingdom on earth, even as we pray that his kingdom come. That is part of what it means to be moral agents, and part of what we ought to do as disciples of Christ. And also part of what the Spirit empowers us to do.

A HINT OF REDEMPTION (OR AT LEAST THE SOFTENING OF A HARD HEART)

The Magician's Nephew has one more reference to Aslan's breath in Chapter 14, the book's penultimate chapter, and this reference is also unique though in a different way. It is the one reference of Aslan's breathing on a character who—up to that point—had made not even a pretense of following Aslan or in any way desiring to do so. Aslan has breathed on characters like Trumpkin who previously had not believed in him, and upon Susan who had gone through a period of stubborn resistance. He will later (in *The Last Battle*) breathe even on Emeth, a Calormene who had considered himself a worshipper of Tash. But each of those characters had, when they finally came to meet Aslan, shown at least some sort of repentance, or belief, or worshipful reverence and fear toward the Great Lion. Uncle Andrew, the titular magician of the story, seems to give no indication of any concerns except how to exploit Narnia (and perhaps

how to dispose of Aslan in order to carry out that exploitation). Aslan himself
makes it clear that Andrew's thoughts have little value. "He thinks great folly,
child," Aslan tells Polly. And he adds that "he has made himself unable to hear
my voice. If I spoke to him, he would hear only growlings and roarings."

So why would Aslan breathe on Andrew? And what (if anything) does that
breath symbolize for readers? I note only that it appears to be at the pleading
of Polly that Aslan intercedes in Uncle Andrew's life, though perhaps he also
does so as a further step to help protect Narnia. Turning to Andrew, Aslan says,
"Oh Adam's sons, how cleverly you defend yourselves against all that might do
you good! But I will give him the only gift he is still able to receive." And then we
read, "He bowed his great head rather sadly, and breathed into the Magician's
terrified face. 'Sleep,' he said. 'Sleep and be separated for some few hours from
all the torments you have devised for yourself.'"

Whatever that breath means, one thing that seems clear is that it is in some
meaningful way a gift to Andrew. Done for Andrew's sake? Or for the sake of
Polly and Digory? Readers are not told. What we do see again is that Aslan is
gentle, even to this unbeliever who is unwilling to listen to his voice. Aslan's
gift to Andrew is a momentary respite from torment. It is a gift of sleep. And if
that breath somehow points us to the power of the Holy Spirit, then this scene
also reflects the small number of passages in the Bible that speak of the Holy
Spirit coming on or somehow inspiring some persons who do not seem to be
following God in any way. (First Samuel 19:19–24 is a favorite example. See also
John 11:49–53.) We are also reminded that the Holy Spirit continues to prompt
unbelievers with opportunities for repentance.

And, indeed, even if Andrew's sleep is only momentary respite, the impact of
Aslan's breath seems to last much longer. It lasts for the rest of Uncle Andrew's
life, in fact. In the final chapter of the book, we read, "Uncle Andrew never tried
any Magic again as long as he lived. He had learned his lesson, and in his old
age he became a nicer and less selfish old man than he had ever been before."
Aslan's breath has a transforming effect. Such a change in Andrew—becoming
nicer and less selfish, and even repenting of his practice of evil magic—is not a
change that is natural. Sin nature would work to make Uncle Andrew steadily
worse. But the Spirit or breath of Aslan bears a different fruit.

VII

THE LAST BATTLE

Beyond Aslan's Breath,
More Pointers to the Holy Spirit

"Then I fell at his feet and thought, Surely this is the hour of death, for the Lion (who is worthy of all honour) will know that I have served Tash all my days and not him," says the Calormene Emeth. "Nevertheless, it is better to see the Lion and die than to be Tisroc of the world and live and not to have seen him."

We have come to the penultimate chapter of *The Last Battle*. We are near the end. The Last Battle has been fought. Night has fallen on Narnia. Though, of course, we are also near the beginning. It is time to go "Further Up and Further In", as the chapter title tells us—to say farewell to the shadowlands. Tirian, Eustace, and Jill are now gathered with Narnia heroes from many of the past stories, including Peter, Edmund, Lucy, Digory, and Polly. Into this company comes a very surprising character, the Calormene Emeth, who proceeds to tell in grand Calormene style the story of his meeting with Aslan—a tale which ends with both an anointing kiss and the breath Aslan.

Exploring *The Magician's Nephew* in the previous chapter, we saw that Aslan's breath (and voice and wind) was present from the start of creation. In *The Last Battle* we find that lion's breath and kiss are mentioned at the end of the world (of Narnia) and the end of time and the start of eternity: "the Great

Story which no one on earth has read: which goes on forever: in which every chapter is better than the one before" (Chapter 16).

Yet Aslan does not actually appear in Narnia in *The Last Battle*. Not even once. That is, he does not appear in the world of the *old* Narnia where most of the scenes of the previous six books have taken place. Characters call to him, hope for him, look for him, and wait for him, but he does not come. Only the false donkey-in-a-lionskin Aslan is present. The real Aslan does not appear until the end of the story when he shows up in the new Narnia. It is there in his own country (or its borderlands) that we get the only two references to Aslan's kiss or breath. One involves several characters (with King Tirian being central), but only Aslan's kiss is mentioned and not his breath. The other involves the Calormene Emeth, whom Aslan welcomes with a kiss and then breathes upon.

THE CALORMENE AND THE KING: ASLAN'S KISS AT THE DOOR TO ETERNITY

The scene involving Emeth, which takes up the first several pages of Chapter 15, offers the only reference to Aslan's breath in *The Last Battle*. Although the scene is described two chapters *after* the other reference to Aslan's kiss, the meeting of Aslan and Emeth seems to have taken place much earlier—before Father Time is awakened and the world of Narnia is brought to an end.

Readers are not told how much time passed between when Emeth entered the stable (which was before the battle) and when he met Aslan. We don't even know what time means or how it passes in Aslan's country. We are told only from two sentences that Emeth "began to journey into the strange country," and "went over much grass and many flowers and among all kinds of wholesome and delectable trees" and then the "great Lion" came to meet him. After meeting Aslan, Emeth spends time wandering the country trying to find him again. Between Emeth entering the stable voluntarily, and Tirian, Jill, and Eustace being forced into it, we have more drama in front of the stable followed by a prolonged battle. So Tirian, Jill, and Eustace come through the stable door long *after* Emeth does. After Aslan greets the others with a kiss, he remains with them and together they watch the drama of the end of time and of old Narnia. It is shortly after this drama and Aslan's disappearance that Emeth appears and tells his story. As I read this, my impression is that not nearly enough time has passed between Aslan's disappearance and Emeth's appearance for the events of Emeth's tale to have unfolded. Why is this important? Perhaps it isn't. Yet it seems to me that Aslan's interaction with Emeth takes place *before* the end of Time, and is the last instance we know of in which he breaths on somebody with intention. Is that because Aslan's deliberate breath—his imparting of his spirit—is no longer needed after the end of time and the start of eternity when all are gathered together in Aslan's kingdom?

As was the case with Eustace's encounter with Aslan on Dragon Island, readers are not present for Emeth's encounter. We only hear about it through his telling. Chapter 15 gives us Emeth's story. After he describes his entry into the stable, and his initial wandering about the land, we come to the point where he describes his meeting with Aslan. Here is a longer part of that tale, with the mention of Aslan's kiss and breath.

> Then I fell at his feet and thought, Surely this is the hour of death, for the Lion (who is worthy of all honour) will know that I have served Tash all my days and not him. Nevertheless, it is better to see the Lion and die than to be Tisroc of the world and live and not to have seen him. But the Glorious One bent down his golden head and touched my forehead with his tongue and said, Son, thou art welcome....
>
> Then he breathed upon me and took away the trembling from my limbs and caused me to stand upon my feet. And after that, he said not much but that we should meet again, and I must go further up and further in. Then he turned him about in a storm and flurry of gold and was gone suddenly.
>
> And since then, O Kings and Ladies, I have been wandering to find him and my happiness is so great that it even weakens me like a wound.

We see yet again the pattern of the lion's kiss, which Emeth describes as a tongue upon his forehead, followed by his breath. As in past scenes, Aslan's kiss and breath strengthen Emeth and take away his fear. After receiving Aslan's breath, Emeth also grows in his desire to know and worship Aslan, as well as in his appreciation for Aslan's love and mercy. Emeth concludes his story (before he is interrupted by the dogs) by adding, "And this is the marvel of marvels, that he called me Beloved."

What I find interesting (and I am by no means the first to do so) is that Aslan breathes on one who had proclaimed himself a follower of Tash. Emeth himself seems surprised that Aslan welcomes him and calls him "Beloved." Given how the narrator has described Emeth's bravery and pursuit of truth (the name *emeth* is a Hebrew word meaning "truth"), and what Jewel had earlier said about him in Chapter 10 ("He is worthy of a better God than Tash"), readers might not be surprised to read of Aslan welcoming him into his kingdom. Yet some Christians may be bothered by it. Was Lewis promoting a doctrine of universal salvation? A close exploration of this is beyond the scope of this book. Suffice it to say that given the scene of judgement that had already taken place (in Chapter 14), Lewis was certainly not promoting universalism.

What the scene does seem to imaginatively illustrate is the Christian doctrine of salvation *by grace,* rather than salvation by correct doctrine. Emeth didn't need to have all the correct answers or a perfectly formed (Trinitarian) theology to be welcomed into Aslan's country. What is clear is that he was a seeker of truth. And more than truth as a mere intellectual idea, he sought to worship one who is truly worthy of worship. Emeth might not have known the name of the true Creator and Ruler of that heavenly kingdom, but he sought him. When he caught a glimpse of Aslan's country, he didn't merely *wish* to know its ruler; he actively searched for him. Though he mistakenly thought he was seeking Tash, he was seeking Aslan all along. And when he met Aslan, he was ready to bow before him. Although Aslan imparts his breath on Emeth in this scene, it seems that Aslan's spirit was working in Emeth all along.

A KISS OF WELCOME AS THE AIR GROWS SWEETER

We turn now to the final scene involving Aslan's kiss—that is, final in terms of Narnian time, though it is described before the scene with Emeth. Although Aslan's name has run throughout *The Last Battle,* and his power has been evident in drawing Jill and Eustace from our world into Narnia, he does not appear until Chapter 13 when the narrative moves from outside the stable to inside, and we find that it is so much bigger on the inside. Infinitely bigger, as it turns out, for the stable door is the door to Aslan's own country: the new Narnia. It is the first step "further up and further in." But the characters don't know this yet. They look around trying to discern where they are.

> The sweet air grew suddenly sweeter. A brightness flashed behind them. All turned. Tirian turned last because he was afraid. There stood his heart's desire, huge and real, the golden Lion, Aslan himself, and already the others were kneeling in a circle round his forepaws and burying their hands and faces in his mane as he stooped his great head to touch them with his tongue. Then he fixed his eyes upon Tirian, and Tirian came near, trembling, and flung himself at the Lion's feet, and the Lion kissed him and said, "Well done, last of the Kings of Narnia who stood firm at the darkest hour."

We see again the kiss of Aslan, first upon the foreheads of the seven kings and queens of Narnia from our world, and then given to Tirian. There is no explicit mention of Aslan's breath, but only a reference to the air growing "suddenly sweeter." In our world, as Christ approached his crucifixion, he told his disciples that he would soon no longer be physically present with them. It was in that context of his impending physical absence that he promised the Holy Spirit. In eternity, Christ's followers will no longer need a special indwelling of the Holy Spirit because we will experience the fullness of God's presence all the time. Sin and sorrow and suffering will be no more. Perhaps for the same reason, in Aslan's Country—when the characters have stepped into eternity— Aslan's breath need no longer be mentioned because Aslan's presence will be be full experienced everywhere. Emeth, entering Aslan's kingdom before the end of time (and becoming one of the few to escape death of his mortal body) might be the last to receive the breath of Aslan because he is the last to need it.

As for Aslan's kiss, might it now turn as much into a kiss of welcome as it is an anointing kiss? There are no more difficult tasks required of Aslan's followers. All that remains is the joy of going "further up and further in." Although perhaps that invitation and journey required its own special anointing, the welcome seems to me to be what is most powerful at this moment. A little later in this chapter, we will consider how, near the start of *The Last Battle,* Tirian was briefly ruled by his anger and how much evil befell because of that. We will also consider how for a time he believed false messages about Aslan because he did not know Aslan as well as he should have. Again, some of the evil may have resulted from that. So often in previous Narnia books, when characters acted unwisely or selfishly or in pride, Aslan prompted them to confess; their confession was part of the process of their spiritual growth. But there is no need for that with Tirian at this point. Evil is gone. Pain and sorrow and loss have passed. It is time for joy. Tirian is welcomed. He has been rewarded. The wrongs he has done are in the past. The good that he did—his standing firm in the last days—remains. The wonderful promise of the Cross is that our sins are forgiven. While Satan acts as accuser, the Holy Spirit confirms our forgiveness.

And that brings us through all the scenes in the Chronicles of Narnia mentioning Aslan's breath or kiss. We could end this book here. Except, as it turns out, there is still more to say about Lewis's portrayal of the Holy Spirit in his Narnia stories.

DIFFERENT EMPHASES, DIFFERENT ANSWERS

In the imagery of Aslan's breath and the associated imagery of his kiss, I have given one answer to the question: "Where and how is the Holy Spirit portrayed in Narnia?" What began for me as an idea, roughly sketched in a talk given virtually in March of 2023, has been fleshed out. But let us now consider again the introduction to this book and the dissatisfaction I expressed with a different answer to the question.

Before turning to Aslan's breath as a primary image pointing readers to the Holy Spirit in Narnia, I suggested that *all* of Aslan's appearances in Narnia following the coronation of the four Pevensies could be considered symbolic of the Holy Spirit. If (as I suggested earlier) we make a connection between Jesus' ascension (forty days after his resurrection and ten days before Pentecost) with Aslan's disappearance at the coronation (following his three-day post-resurrection presence in Narnia), then that earlier answer has some appeal. After all, the Holy Spirit remained present on earth in and with Jesus' followers, but Jesus himself (God the Son) was no longer *bodily* present.

My dissatisfaction with that answer stemmed from both a theological point and a literary interest in the imagery. The theological point was an emphasis on the Trinity. Christians understand Father, Son, and Holy Spirit to be three distinct persons. Jesus himself referenced this clearly in his well-known Great Commission when commanded his followers to make disciples and to baptize them "in the name of the Father and of the Son and of the Holy Spirit" (Matthew 28:19). That emphasis on three persons is what initially prompted the question about portrayals of the Holy Spirit in the Chronicles of Narnia—the question that led to this book. As the New Testament reveals distinct persons in Jesus and the Heavenly Father whom Jesus often spoke of, spoke to, and claimed to reveal, so also does C.S. Lewis portray Aslan and the Emperor-beyond-the-Sea as distinct persons in the Narnia stories. So what of the person of the Holy Spirit?

From a literary viewpoint, I was looking for a portrayal that was also neatly represented in the imagery. And Aslan's breath, as distinct from Aslan himself, satisfies that. It works. I believe it works well; especially combined with his kiss, the imagery of Aslan's breath provides many pointers to and thoughtful reflections on the Holy Spirit and his work in the world. As I wrote this book, I found myself often pausing to reflect on Lewis's insights and being challenged or encouraged by them.

Yet we might approach this entire question with a different emphasis. What

if instead of emphasizing the three *distinct* persons of the Holy Spirit, we empha-
sized instead the *oneness* of God? After all, the Trinitarian understanding of God
as three persons still affirms that there is only one God. The Holy Trinity is not
some equivalent to Odin, Thor, and Loki, or to Jupiter, Mars, and Apollo, or to any
other trio of man-made deities. Father, Son, and Holy Spirit are (in some mysterious way that I can affirm but cannot fully grasp) one God. The Holy Spirit in us *is*
Christ in us. Christ with us *is* also the Holy Spirit with us. Likewise, as Jesus told
both his followers and those who opposed him, if we know the Son then we know
the Father, and if we know the Father then we know the Son (John 1:18; 8:19;
10:30; 14:8–20, etc.) So even if Aslan's breath is a central metaphor or symbol in
the Narnia stories pointing to the person of the Holy Spirit, it is also fully appropriate that Lewis's portrayal of Aslan himself (and not just his breath)—especially
his post-ascension appearances—might also give insight into what Lewis thought
of the Holy Spirit, and also how the Holy Spirit works in us and in the world.

There is at least one more hint in Lewis's stories that this might be the
case—one I never considered until I was halfway through writing this book and
was rereading more closely some of the important passages in *The Silver Chair*.
Many older readers may remember that the Greek phrase *pnuema hagion,*
which is rendered as "Holy Spirit" in most modern New Testament translations,
was translated as "Holy Ghost" in the original King James Version (KJV). In the
New King James Version (NKJV), the translators revised that to "Holy Spirit,"
but that newer translation did not appear until after the death of C.S. Lewis.
Lewis grew up with the original KJV (also known as the Authorized Version[10])
and thus also with the New Testament title *Holy Ghost* for the Third Person of
the Trinity. Although I was born the year that Lewis died and am more familiar
with modern translations than with the KJV, I still grew up singing (and still at
times sing) a doxology that begins "Praise God from whom all blessings flow,"
and ends with "Praise Father, Son, and Holy Ghost."

---

10 Although C.S. Lewis pointed out that for most modern readers the archaic language of the KJV
could easily be misunderstood, and that as English (and other languages) continually change there
was regular ongoing needs for new translations of the Bible, as a Renaissance literature scholar he
appreciated the KJV and was very familiar with it. He even gave a lecture (later published as a book)
on its literary impact. For more on this topic, see "Modern Translations of the Bible" in *God in the
Dock: Essays on Theology and Ethics* and *The Literary Impact of the Authorized Version,* both by Lewis.

Why is this important? There is an interesting dialogue in the final chapter of *The Silver Chair* when Caspian is brought back to life in Aslan's country. At first, Jill and Eustace are afraid that Caspian might be a ghost since they saw him die. Caspian replies, "You think I'm a ghost.... But don't you see? I would be that if I appeared in Narnia now: because I don't belong there any more. But one can't be a ghost in one's own country." While Caspian can now claim the country they are in as the place he *belongs* and where he is *not* a ghost, readers know the place to be Aslan's Country. And immediately before Caspian speaks, Aslan made the comment, "Most people have [died], you know. Even I have." What if we put together Aslan's reference to his own death and Caspian's comment about ghosts? Then it would follow that while Aslan himself would not be a ghost in his own country, he *would* be a ghost if he appeared in Narnia! Or we might more accurately say, he would be the Holy Ghost!

Of course, Aslan has appeared in Narnia. He has done so repeatedly through the stories that follow *The Lion, the Witch and the Wardrobe* through Narnian history. Thus, the possible answer I found unsatisfying at the start of this book—and which I still find unsatisfying in terms of literary imagery—may be an important part of a much bigger and more comprehensive answer after all. And while I am appreciative of Lewis's more overt imagery of Aslan's breath and kiss (and found it worth a careful exploration), we should consider this bigger picture. For even as Aslan's sacrifice on the Stone Table may point readers to Christ's death on the cross, so also the portrayal of Aslan's comings and goings and interactions in Narnia after that death and resurrection also point readers to the *character* and *work* of the Holy Spirit. Indeed, Lewis's portrayal of the Holy Spirit (which many readers have thought to be absent) may be the richest and most evident of any of the portrayals of the three persons of the Trinity.

For me, the most important aspect of all of this is the personal and relational aspect. Aslan appears to individual persons, and interacts with them *as individuals.* He cares for the unique story of each person (and is careful when speaking with one person not to answer questions about the stories of others). In his introduction to *Christ Plays in Ten Thousand Places,* Eugene Peterson wrote the following:

"Trinity" is the theological formulation that most adequately provides a structure of keeping conversations on the Christian life coherent, focused, and personal. Early on the Christian community realized that everything about us—our worshiping and learning, conversing and listening, teaching and preaching, obeying and deciding, working and playing, eating and sleeping—takes place in the "country" of the Trinity, that is in the presence and among the operations of God the Father, God the Son, and God the Holy Spirit. . . . Trinity is a conceptual attempt to provide coherence to God as God is revealed variously as Father, Son, and Holy Spirit in our Scriptures: God is emphatically *personal;* God is only and exclusively God in *relationship.* Trinity is not an attempt to explain or define God by means of abstractions (although there is some of that, too), but a witness that God reveals himself as personal and in personal relations. . . . God is . . . brought boldly into a community of men, women, and children who are called to enter into this communal life of love, an emphatically *personal* life where they experience themselves in personal terms of love and forgiveness, of hope and desire. Under the image of the Trinity we discover that we do not know God by defining him but by being loved by him and loving in return. (6–7)

This is a description of a Trinitarian God—Father, Son, and Holy Spirit—at work within us. Jesus said he would be present in and with his disciples through the promised Holy Spirit, even as he told them that they could know the Father by knowing the Son. Again, putting aside my desire for particular imagery related to the Holy Spirit, it is quite reasonable that in his Narnia stories Lewis might also portray God's continued work in his people through Aslan himself even when the Scriptures attribute that work specifically to the person of the Holy Spirit.

This is especially true of the personal aspect of the Holy Spirit's work in our lives, and of our personal relationship with God through the Spirit. The Spirit is with us when we are walking along a road (even a road through the mountains at night, or through a land full of giants.) He is with us in a strange city, or when we journey through a forest full of enemies who are sending arrows at us. He is with us when we must cross a desert (including both the literal and metaphorical kind). And He is with us both when we are alone and when we are feasting and celebrating with friends. The Spirit is with us when we have forgotten his ways and need a reminder, when we are fearful and need courage, when we are sad and need comfort, and when our hearts have turned toward the golden statues (or lion-skin-covered false gods) of this world. Which is to say, the Holy Spirit is with us in the same sorts of places that Aslan appears in the Narnia stories set in the latter days.

Consider as an example one important and beloved scene involving a post-ascension appearance of Aslan: the un-dragoning of Eustace on Dragon Island in Chapter 7 of *The Voyage of the Dawn Treader*. We considered this scene only briefly in Chapter 3 since it does not explicitly mention Aslan's breath or kiss, but it is worth returning to as it provides an excellent example of how Lewis's portrayal of the post-ascension Aslan himself (and not just his breath) may provide imagery of, pointers to, or insights into the Holy Spirit and his work.

Lewis does not present the scene in the present tense, but through the latter narration of Eustace to Edmund, with Edmund as a more knowledgeable and trustworthy presence to help interpret Eustace's experience for him, and also for readers. Eustace describes a huge lion calling him to follow, but then—upon Edmund's questioning of this point, "You mean it spoke?" —realizes that that the lion didn't actually speak: "Now that you mention it, I don't think it did. But it told me all the same." A little later, Eustace emphasizes the same point again. "But the lion told me I must undress first. Mind you, I don't know if he said any words out loud or not." This seems a wonderful metaphor for how the Holy Spirit often speaks to those who follow Christ. For example, Paul writes in his epistles of Christians being "led by the Spirit" (Romans 8:14; Galatians 5:18), yet I venture to say that for most of us, most of the time, even when that leading is clear it rarely comes in audible words. When the Second Person of the Trinity is incarnate in the person of Jesus, he speaks frequently to his followers, but he does so using a real flesh-and-blood voice, with human vocal chords producing physical vibrations in the air that reach the ear drums of listeners. He does so as they eat meals together, or walk together along dusty roads beneath the Judean sunlight. The book of Acts, however, often presents the Holy Spirit communicating without any specific words being recorded—possibly without audible words even being spoken—and yet in a way that is clearly understood, much like we see in this scene in which Aslan communicates personally with Eustace.

And also in a relational way; the interactions of both the incarnate Son of God and of the Holy Spirit are personal and relational. And just as the instruction of Jesus was often "follow me", so also the Spirit's message is often an instruction to go (or not to go) to some particular place (See Acts 8:29, 13:4, 16:6-7, 20:22.)

There is also much in the scene that reveals a supernatural power. Aslan leads Eustace to a mountaintop garden that didn't seem to have existed before. Eustace, despite his flying all over the island in dragon form, had never seen the place. It isn't merely the garden that he hadn't seen (which wouldn't be surprising for a small garden in a vast wilderness) but the entire mountain seems not to have been present. And after his un-dragoning, Eustace is mysteriously and "suddenly" transported back to the beach in a way that—even more than Jill's cross-ocean journey on Aslan's breath—is reminiscent of the Holy Spirit whisking Philip away from the Ethiopian eunuch. It is also so supernatural that Eustace wonders if the entire experience might have been a dream, but the wiser Edmund is adamant that it was not, and provides good evidence for that conclusion.

None of this in and of itself is particularly important. They may be hints about C.S.Lewis's literary imagery and how it points to Biblical portrayals of and teachings about the Holy Spirit. What is far more important, though, is what Aslan does and doesn't do in this scene, and what Eustace can and cannot do, and the deeper truths these observations provide. Early in this book as I wrote about spiritual renewal and spiritual transformation, I pointed out in the Biblical language—especially Paul's use of the passive voice to give instructions in his epistles—that this renewal and transformation is something we cannot do in ourselves, and yet it is something we are called to participate in. Or, we might say, we are called to yield to that work. God seems to have given us the freedom to say "no" to his work; he chooses not to work in our lives unless we allow him. This is precisely what Lewis illustrations in the un-dragoning of Eustace. It is a wonderful metaphor for spiritual transformation. Eustace cannot remove his old dragon skin. No effort of his own will accomplish that. Only Aslan can do it. Yet Aslan waits until Eustace willingly submits. And the process of transformation, we learn, is painful. "It hurt worse than anything I've ever felt," Eustace says. For me the most telling phrase in Eustace's description is when he describes Aslan's claws as having "gone right into my heart." Isn't that the transformation we all need? A changing of our heart? Our own efforts address only superficial actions. We might address some outward habit, or outward sin—the outer layer of our dragon skin—but eventually the inward heart will always break through. Until our heart is changed, we will not be fundamentally transformed. Only the Holy Spirit can change our hearts, and that change is precisely what God offers if we are willing to submit to it: to "just lay flat down" on our backs and "let him do it" as Eustace did. The baptism imagery that follows (remember that John the Baptist spoke of Messiah as one who would baptize with the Holy Spirit) and the re-clothing of Eustace are beautiful also.

We could turn from this example to any of the multiple appearances of Aslan everywhere. From the perspective of Shasta in *The Horse and His Boy*, there seemed to be "so many lions" (Chapter 11). Why? Because Aslan was constantly involved in Shasta's story and (like the Holy Spirit) was present with him through his whole life. Aslan spoke with Lucy on her journey from Cair Paravel to Aslan's Howe, and again in the house of Coriakin (after which he went off to see Tumnus). He makes a personal visit to Aravis, Hwin, and Bree at the Hermit's house. In his jaunt across Narnia with Lucy and Susan in *Prince Caspian*, he also visits Gwendolen and the ill "Auntie" with dwarf-blood (Caspian's former nurse) whom he heals and then gives a ride to. Each visit is personal, and also in some ways healing or redemptive. We did not explore many of these in this book because they did not involve Aslan's breath or kiss, but we could have commented on them all with respect to the Holy Spirit.

Consider too the many appearances in which Aslan is invisible, or appears in dreams, or quickly disappears. This book has mentioned several such appearances: to Lucy in the pages of the Coriakin's magic book, to Caspian in his cabin, to Jill in the Giant's house, and possibly also on Deathwater Island to Lucy, Caspian, Edmund, Eustace, and Reepicheep. Our earlier emphasis was on what Aslan said or did in that dream and particularly on his breath and kiss. In the context of the symbolism of his breath, that made sense. Yet we could also consider the simple fact that these characters had dreams and visions of Aslan in the first place, apart from the specific content of these dreams. Through the prophet Joel, God promises,

And afterward,
I will pour out my Spirit on all people.
Your sons and daughters will prophesy,
your old men will dream dreams,
your young men will see visions.
Even on my servants, both men and women,
I will pour out my Spirit in those days. (Joel 2:28–29)

In his Pentecost sermon, Peter quotes from this passage (Acts 2:16–21.) Joel tells us—and Peter reminds us—that dreams and visions are signs of the presence of the Spirit of God "pour[ed] out" on people. Thus, when Lewis showed Aslan appearing in dreams and visions, apart from any reference to his breath or kiss, Lewis was (intentionally or not) drawing on biblical pointers to the Holy Spirit right from the day of Pentecost.

In *Christ Plays in Ten Thousand Places,* Eugene Peterson comments on the significance of the biblical words used for Spirit in Hebrew and Greek (in a passage which provided a primary hint for this book):

> Living, living fully and well, is at the heart of all serious spirituality. "Spirit," in our three parent languages of Hebrew, Greek, and Latin, carries with it the root meaning of breath and easily offers itself up as a metaphor for life. . . . [T]he spirit is God's spirit: God alive, God creating, God saving, God blessing. God lives and gives life. God lives and brims with life. God lives and permeates everything we see and hear and taste and touch, everything we experience. (29)

As noted above, this description of the Spirit could be a description of Aslan in Narnia. And as the title *Christ Plays in Ten Thousand Places* really addresses the work of the Holy Spirit though history and in our own lives, so we might note that Aslan's repeated appearances in so many places in the Narnia stories—even without mention of his breath—is also a pointer to the work of the Holy Spirit in Narnian history and in the lives of its characters.

LISTENING FOR PROMPTS

It was as I started writing *Aslan's Breath* that I also started reading Peterson's book. I had no particular plan to do so, or to quote from any works of theology, even as I have also resisted drawing from the wealth of excellent scholarship on C.S. Lewis and the Chronicles of Narnia. But then I sensed a prompting—without any reason why—that it was time to pick up that book off my shelf: one of only two remaining Peterson books in my collection I had not previously read.

Almost at once, I began to see connections to my writing about the Holy Spirit in Narnia. Peterson describes his book as a work of *spiritual theology*. It is about spirituality: not spirituality in a vague secular sense, or even a vague religious sense, but spirituality in the specific sense of a life lived in the power of the Holy Spirit. Not surprisingly (though I didn't realize this before I began it), the person and work of the Holy Spirit is thus a central topic in *Christ Plays in Ten Thousand Places*. It was perhaps the most timely book I could have begun. I would be thinking and writing about a particular passage in the Chronicles of Narnia and the next day I'd come upon a passage in Peterson's book that would trigger all sorts of ideas and insights. Or sometimes I would read a passage from Peterson's book first, and the next day a scene from Narnia resonated closely with it.

That raises an interesting question that relates to *Aslan's Breath*—and a topic with which I end my own book. How do we recognize the voices, urgings, or nudges of the Holy Spirit? How do we listen *for* and *to* that still small voice: that gentle whisper that is neither an earthquake, nor a fire, nor a raging wind? I don't think I recognized a "prompting" to read *Christ Plays in Ten Thousand Places* as coming from the Holy Spirit when I picked it up and started it. Even now, I can't assuredly claim it was. I only know that Peterson's book has helped me grow in my thinking about God, in my participation in the Holy Spirit's work in my life, and (I think and hope) writing a stronger book about the Narnia stories. Often, however, it *is* important to discern whether a voice we hear is coming from the Holy Spirit or from the world, because discerning whose voice is speaking in turn informs us whether or not to follow that voice. God's voice is rarely a shout. He does not force us to obey him. He gives us the freedom to turn away. Yet he constantly calls us to himself.

That question leads us back to the Chronicles of Narnia and specifically to *The Last Battle*—not merely to the imagery of Aslan's breath, but to the rest of the story, when Aslan doesn't seem to be present. In many ways, the examples of visits from Aslan over the first six books begin to answer that question of how to recognize his voice, but it is in *The Last Battle* that these lessons take on new weight. They do so precisely because Aslan is *not* visibly present. Characters (and readers) must learn to discern his voice even when they (and we) cannot see him.

As we have already seen in the six earlier books, Aslan does many things in his personal visits. He is a comforter. He helps free people from fear. When the protagonists (mostly children) have done wrong, Aslan calls them to acknowledge their errors. He guides and directs his followers, even as he strengthens and emboldens them. He also often prompts characters to choose the right path: the way of following him rather than the ways of the world, though the latter are often easier or more appealing. Aslan does these things whether his voice or kiss are specifically mentioned or not. And in each of these ways, Aslan's work in Narnia is very much like that of the Holy Spirit in our lives.

Consider for a moment just the last of these: reminding characters what is right and wrong and what *ought* to be done, and encouraging them along that right path. We might think of these visits by or visions of Aslan as promptings, but Aslan still leaves the final choice of what to do up to the character. He never takes away free will. He helps Eustace *understand* how to get out of his dragon skin, and is ready to help when Eustace is ready to receive the help (since it is not something Eustace can do alone), but he does not force the decision on Eustace. We observe something similar with Lucy when Aslan asks her to wake her siblings in *Prince Caspian,* or again in *The Voyage of the Dawn Treader* when she considers reading in Coriakin's book "An infallible spell to make beautiful her that uttereth it beyond the lot of mortals" (Chapter 10). And with Caspian in his cabin when he is in a fit of stubborn pride. And so on. Aslan may point characters along the right road, but he does not force them to take that road.

Similarly, he often prompts characters to acknowledge their own wrongdoings and to make their own confessions, but he leaves it to them to do so. All of these are promptings to listen to his ways and follow him. They are like the promptings of the Holy Spirit to follow the way of Christ. But here is the thing: in all the aforementioned examples, Aslan is recognizable *as Aslan.* That doesn't mean it is easy for the children to obey him or follow his path or confess their wrongs. They often struggle, and Aslan's breath often helps them with that struggle. Yet for the most part—particularly with those characters who know

Aslan and have in the past made a choice to follow him—the struggle is *not* one of recognizing or knowing who is speaking to them; it is the struggle of whether to obey and yield to his will.

RECOGNIZING ASLAN'S VOICE WHEN HE IS NOT VISIBLY PRESENT

In *The Last Battle,* however, Aslan does *not* appear. Neither Tirian nor Jill or Eustace see him or speak with him. In many ways, that makes the situation in that final story more like what many of us face today. Characters may experience a sort of prompting to act a certain way, but there is no visible lion standing beside them speaking in an audible voice. One of the most important instances arises with Puzzle in the first chapter of the book when Shift suggests to him a plan to put on a lion skin and pretend to be Aslan. Puzzle must discern between two voices. One voice is the ape's, which is loud and demanding. Shift tells Puzzle, "Probably [Aslan] sent us the lion-skin on purpose, so that we could set things to right. Anyway, he never does turn up, you know. Not now-a-days." Here are two contradictory arguments, both of which are common in the world. One argument tries to conflate a personal desire with the will of God: the thing we want to do must be God's will. (Conveniently enough, God's supposed will often makes the preacher of that message wealthier.) The other argument suggests that God's will doesn't even matter because God isn't really present. (This is the argument that there is no meaningful morality.) Shift simultaneously takes both approaches at once with Puzzle.

The other prompting that Puzzle senses is not audible at all; it is Puzzle's own conscience speaking to him the truth about Aslan. "I knew we were doing something dreadfully wicked," he tells Shift. "Take this wretched skin off me at once." I have always understood the "great thunderclap right overhead" and the "small earthquake" that flings the two characters on their faces, and which precede Puzzle's thought, as a sign from Aslan. Not a still small voice at all! Yet signs in nature can be difficult to interpret, or even to know whether they are signs at all or merely natural phenomena. Aslan is not visibly present to interpret it, and Shift interprets it the opposite way Puzzle does, leaving Puzzle still with the task of discerning which voice to listen to: that of Shift, or that which comes from his knowledge of Aslan's character (and of right and wrong). Had Shift listened to the moral prompting, the disaster that fell upon Narnia might well have been averted. Instead, Puzzle chose to be a people-pleaser—or, rather, an ape-pleaser.

In the next chapter, titled tellingly "The Rashness of the King," King Tirian must also discern between two promptings when he hears of the evil befalling the dryads. In his case, it is the audible voice of the centaur Roonwit that is the prompting of wisdom. "Sire, be wary even in your just wrath. There are strange doings on foot. If there should be rebels in arms further up the valley, we three are too few to meet them. If it would please you to wait while—"

Roonwit's words and prompting of wisdom are cut off because Tirian does not even give this first voice a chance to finish. The other prompting is the louder voice of his own anger. "For a moment the King's grief and anger were so great that he could not speak," the narrator tells us. A little later we read, "The King was still so angry." And still later, "He did not see at the moment how foolish it was for two of them to go alone; nor did the King. They were too angry to think clearly. But much evil came of their rashness in the end." And finally, "there came over him and over Jewel such a rage that they did not know what they were doing."

It might be rather tedious to examine every example where a character needs discernment to recognize the voice or nudging of Aslan. Even Professor Digory responds to "a feeling that we were somehow wanted [in Narnia]" (Chapter 5). But one such category of examples is central to the entire story. Through the first several chapters of *The Last Battle,* Narnians are repeatedly given words or orders purportedly coming from Aslan. The response of the water rats when asked by Tirian (in Chapter 2) why they are hauling logs down the river becomes a sort of refrain through the story: "The Lion's orders, Sire. Aslan himself." Only a chapter later, the horses say something similar in answer to Tirian's question "how came these aliens to enslave you?" Their reply: "Aslan is here. It is all by his orders." The question Tirian asks after hearing the answer of the water rats in many ways gets at the heart of the type of discernment we need, and leads us to the central point of this section. "'Aslan,' said the King at last, in a very low voice. 'Aslan. Could it be true? Could he be felling the holy trees and murdering the Dryads?'"

Lewis leaves readers with little doubt about Tirian's character: that if the real Aslan had appeared at that moment, the Narnian king would have obeyed him. Yet unlike many famous scenes in the previous Narnia stories, Aslan does not appear (despite the repeated requests and desire of the characters to see him and hear him). How often I would like to hear God's voice speak more clearly in my life and make some difficult decision easier! It can be difficult to discern what prompts and nudging come to us from the Holy Spirit.

But Lewis does suggest some help for us. Tirian asks, "Could [Aslan] be felling the holy trees and murdering the Dryads?" I suspect that nearly anyone who has read the entire series and comes to that point in the tale knows the answer; it is a resounding "no." Neither would Aslan order the sale of any Narnian creature (nor even any Calormene) into slavery. Nor would Aslan endorse the poverty of the squirrels so that Shift, their self-appointed religious leader, could grow wealthy at their expense. Aslan repeatedly reveals himself through the Narnia stories—both to readers and to characters within the tale—as a comforter. And gentleness is central to his character: he does not put it on or off like a cloak when it is convenient. His is a profound gentleness saturated with mercy that is expressed even to characters like the dragon Eustace, and the traitor Edmund, and the dwarfs who refused to be taken in, and even Uncle Andrew. The ape Shift threatens the animals, saying "Aslan says he's been far too soft with you before, do you see? Well, he isn't going to be soft any more. He's going to lick you into shape this time." Even though Aslan is not visibly present, all those who know him—both readers and characters within the story—should recognize this as a lie not in keeping with Aslan's character.

And now I'm plunged back into the earlier stories for a moment. Was it easier for Lucy to discern Aslan's leading because she saw him? My first answer is yes. It probably was. But then I think of characters like Digory's uncle Andrew in *The Magician's Nephew* or the dwarves in the stable at the end of *The Last Battle*. Those who don't know and trust Aslan are not helped by his presence (even when he is gentle with them). Seeing him does not suddenly enable them to recognize his voice. Lucy sees and hears Aslan precisely because she *does* know him. Had Tirian known Aslan better—had any of the animals at the Stable known Aslan better—he (and they) might more quickly have realized that the Ape's message was not the true voice of Aslan. I think of other times when characters must discern between multiple voices. Caspian hears the voice of Nikabrik telling him that political power is what is important: the power to overthrow his enemies. And if bringing the White Witch back will give them power, then it is the best thing to do. The quieter voice says to trust Aslan rather than seeking power through worldly means.

How do we recognize the promptings of Holy Spirit and distinguish that voice from the many voices of the world—which are often much louder? Lewis's stories suggest at least a few answers. We might ask whether the voice promotes fear or frees us from fear. So many voices in our culture today do the former: news media, social media, politicians—even some church pastors and religious leaders. Shift promotes fear because his power comes from fear. He uses the name of Aslan to promote fear. By contrast, the real Aslan repeatedly frees us from fear.

Or we might ask whether the voice speaks of the value of *all* life? Does it promote justice and turn us away from anything that is oppressive? Does the voice call us to gentleness, or does it speak of gentleness as an old-fashioned virtue that can be cast aside when it no longer seems to gain us power?

I also think of how when Tirian was ruled by the voice of his anger, he ignored the voice of Roonwit: a voice that had proven to be knowledgeable and wise in the ways of Aslan and creation; a voice that was known to be trustworthy; a voice Tirian *should* have listened to instead of cutting it short. When we listen for the Holy Spirit, do we pay attention to the godly voices of wisdom in our lives? Or do we (like Tirian) listen to our anger, or (like Puzzle) to voices of greed and self-interest?

Ultimately, the best way to discern the voices of the true Aslan from the wearers of lion-skins is to know Aslan better. Any voice that comes from Aslan should point us back toward Aslan and his character and teachings. Aslan's breath carries the very scent of Aslan. Those who seek Aslan should listen to his voice, know him, and be present and still before him so that we might experience his breath and anointing kiss upon ourselves.

Further Up and Further In

Below is a short list of recommended readings for those interested in a deeper (and more scholarly) exploration of the Chronicles of Narnia (especially its spiritual and theological themes), and in the life and spiritual journey of C.S.Lewis. There are many other excellent sources worth of recommendation beyond those in this short list. Indeed, one could fill a book just listing books, book chapters, and essays about C.S.Lewis or the Chronicles of Narnia.

Downing, David, *Into the Wardrobe: C. S. Lewis and the Narnia Chronicles,* Hoboken: Josey-Bass, 2005.

Ford, Paul, *Companion to Narnia, Revised Edition: A Complete Guide to the Magical World of C.S. Lewis's The Chronicles of Narnia,* New York: Macmillan, 1985.

> Paul Ford's important work—which (to my embarrassment) I did not have a copy of and had not read prior to my writing of this book—is of particular note in this list. Ford's comprehensive exploration does indeed have an entry on "Holy Spirit," and within that entry's several paragraphs, one mentions Aslan's breath as "the chief symbol of the spirit's activity" (p. 230) and provides a list of some examples, while another paragraph mentions the wind in *The Magician's Nephew.* Ford also suggests some other symbols of the Spirit which I had not considered, such as the gifts of Father Christmas to three of the Pevensies and the sweet waters of the Last Sea which he refers to as "one of the most striking images of the Spirit's activity" (p. 231).

Glyer, Diana Pavlac, *The Company They Keep: C.S.Lewis and J.R.R.Tolkien as Writers in Community,* Kent: Kent State University Press, 2007.

Hooper, Walter, *Past Watchful Dragons: The Origin. Interpretation, and Appreciation of the Chronicles of Narnia,* Eugene: Wipf and Stock, 2007.

Jacobs, Alan, T*he Narnian: The Life and Imagination of C.S.Lewis,* San Francisco: HarperSanFrancisco, 2005.

Michael Ward, *Planet Narnia: The Seven Heavens in the Imagination of C. S. Lewis,* Oxford: Oxford University Press, 2010.

Williams, Donald T., *Deeper Magic: The Theology Behind the Writings of C.S.Lewis,* Baltimore: Square Halo Books: 2016.

Acknowledgements

I am appreciative of the wonderful community of writers I have in the Chrysostom Society, the community of fellow believers I have at Memorial Baptist Church in Middlebury (especially my Wednesday morning prayer group and Rev. Dr. Allen for our regular conversations about theology, literature, faith, and culture), the community of thoughtful readers and scholars I have found in the Inklings Folk Fellowship (especially Joe Ricke, who brought the group together and provides leadership), and the New York C.S. Lewis Society for listening to me present an early version of my exploration of Aslan's breath and encouraging me to turn those ideas into this book. Thanks also to Joseph Milligan, Kevin Belmonte, and Brenton Dickieson for reading a draft of this book and offering helpful feedback.

Special thanks to my wonderful wife, Deborah, and my sons and daughters-in-law Thomas and Courtney, Mark and Ellie, and Peter and McKenna, who have supported and encouraged my writing over the years, and who have put up with way too many (and too often repeated) dinner conversations about my observations on various works of literature.

—Matthew Dickerson
Summer, 2023

Works Cited

Lewis, C.S.
—*The Lion, the Witch and the Wardrobe.* New York: Macmillian, 1950.
—*Prince Caspian.* New York: Macmillian, 1951.
—*The Voyage of the Dawn Treader.* New York: Macmillian, 1952.
—*The Silver Chair.* New York: Macmillian, 1953.
—*The Horse and His Boy.* New York: Macmillian, 1954.
—*The Magician's Nephew.* New York: Macmillian, 1955.
—*The Last Battle.* New York: Macmillian, 1956.
—*That Hideous Strength.* New York: Simon and Schuster, 1996.
—*The Abolition of Man.* New York: Touchstone, 1996.
—*That Hideous Strength.* New York: Scribner, 1996.
—*Surprised by Joy.* San Francisco: HarperOne, 2017.
—"The Efficacy of Prayer" in *The World's Last Night and Other Essays.* San Diego: Harcourt, 1960. 3–11.

Peterson, Eugene. *Christ Plays in Ten Thousand Places: A Conversation in Spiritual Theology.* Grand Rapids, MI: Eerdmans, 2005.

Tolkien, J.R.R.
—*The Fellowship of the Ring.* Boston: Houghton Mifflin, 1981.
—*The Return of the King.* Boston: Houghton Mifflin, 1981.
—*The Letters of J. R. R. Tolkien.* Selected and edited by Humphrey Carpenter, with the assistance of Christopher Tolkien. Boston: Houghton Mifflin, 1981.

Selected Other Works
by Matthew Dickerson

RELATED TO C.S. LEWIS AND J.R.R. TOLKIEN

—(*With David O'Hara*), *From Homer to Harry Potter: A Handbook on Myth and Fantasy*. Grand Rapids: Brazos Press, 2006.

—(*With Jonathan Evans*) *Ents, Elves, and Eriador: The Environmental Vision of J.R.R. Tolkien*. Lexington: University Press of Kentucky, 2006.

—(*With David O'Hara*) *Narnia and the Fields of Arbol: The Environmental Vision of C.S. Lewis*. Lexington: University Press of Kentucky, 2009.

—*A Hobbit Journey: Discovering the Enchantment of J.R.R. Tolkien's Middle-earth*. Grand Rapids: Brazos Press, 2012.

—*The Mind and the Machine: What it Means to be Human and Why it Matters*. Revised 2nd edition. Eugene: Cascade Press, 2016.

FROM SQUARE HALO BOOKS

—"Fantasy" in *A Book for Hearts and Minds: What You Should Read & Why*. Baltimore: Square Halo Books, 2017.

—"Tolkien, Creativity, Mortality, Fall" in *J.R.R. Tolkien and the Arts: A Theology of Subcreation*. Baltimore: Square Halo Books, 2021.

—"Sorrow and Grace in Tolkien's Works" in *Wild Things and Castles in the Sky: A Guide to Choosing the Best Books for Children*. Baltimore: Square Halo Books, 2021.

WORKS OF FICTION

—*The Finnsburg Encounter*. Wheaton: Crossway Books, 1991.

—*The Rood and the Torc: The Song of Kristinge, Son of Finn*. San Antonio: Wings Press, 2014.

—*The Gifted*. Chattanooga: AMG, 2015.

RELATED TO NATURE AND OUTDOORS

—*The Voices of Rivers: Reflections on Places Wild and Almost Wild*. Pawcatuck: Homebound Publications, 2019.

—*A Fine-Spotted Trout on Corral Creek: on the Cutthroat Competition of the Native Trout of the Northern Rockies*. San Antonio: Wings Press, 2021.

—*The Salvelinus, the Sockeye, and the Egg-Sucking Leech: Abundance and Diversity in the Bristol Bay Drainage (from the Eyes of an Angler)*. San Antonio: Wings Press, 2023.